Money Makers

The Easiest Way to Build a Business WITHOUT Paid Ads or a Big Following

Dr. Izdihar Jamil, Ph.D.

Publishing History

Paperback Edition 1 / February 2022
ISBN: 978-1-4583-8315-0
Imprint: M&S Publishing

DR IZDIHAR JAMIL, PH.D.
MEDIA EXPERT

Dedication

Thank you, Tomel, for showing Mommy the true meaning of miracles. And to all who are fighting the good fight – one step at a time and keep moving forward.

You've got this!

Reviews

"In *Money Makers*, Dr. Jamil gives actionable advice about how you can create an online business that actually makes good money! I love how she gets specific about what you need to do. She describes how her first attempt to sell an online course did not go well and how she figured out what she needed to change to create sales. It is inspiring how Dr. Jamil empowers people to create financial freedom."

Dr. Kathleen Wright-Knothe, Psychologist and High Performance Coach

"That's a nice, concise overview of social media platforms. I like your calls to action!"

Barbara Norman, CFP

"As an entrepreneur, this book has hit home for me. It's never about the business owner; it's about serving your clients and their needs. Izdihar shares the magical formula that has helped her master the strategies for her success."

Michelle Mehta, Confidence Expert

"I highly recommend this book! It provides simple and effective ways to market your expertise, build your clientele, and gain profit WITHOUT paid ads. A practical and valuable strategy to Grow your Business!"

Dr. Veronica Joseph, #1 International Best-Selling Author of *Unlocking Your Super Life* and Holistic Wellness Expert

"This book is amazing and right on point. There is so much goodness here. I love how you explain the action plans inside each chapter and then summarize them with a Call to Action. Amazing! I loved reading this book!"

Lisa Stern, Health Coach

Reviews

"If it were not for Dr. Izdihar Jamil's business savvy and her proven approach, I would not have become an Amazon #1 International Best-Selling Author. Dr. Jamil is both relatable and an inspiration. Having worked closely with her, I can tell you that I was surprised to learn of her humble beginnings. This book describes in detail her journey from the shadows into the *Spotlight* of success. Izdihar's advice is not only effective for established professionals but for anyone just starting out. My favorite quote from her book is, 'Before, I was lost within thousands of other coaches and consultants. Now, I stand out because I choose to own the spotlight.' ~ Dr. Izdihar Jamil. *Money Makers,* is a must read, especially if you want to enjoy the spotlight.

Deb Rosman, author of *The Grieving Heart: A Collection of Poetry and Prose* about Loss, Hope and Living, and an Amazon #1 International Best-Selling Author, of *It is Done!*.

Table of Contents

Preface

I know the world of entrepreneurship can be a scary place to be, especially if you come from a family that is very successful in their 9-5 jobs. And when you do jump into the business world, you are bombarded with so many unnecessary things, and you end up spending thousands of dollars even before your business begins. I think that's crazy!

That's the whole reason why I wanted to write this book. I wanted to show you the simplicity of building and scaling your business. Once you master these fundamentals, you can make money even without the use of fancy technology or expensive advertisements.

Today, I have built my business without spending any money on advertisements. I didn't even have complicated funnels (I didn't even know what it was, too!) or have fancy websites when I first started. But I was still able to make money in my business by mastering organic methods.

I did all that while taking care of three young children. The key to a successful business is knowing exactly what you need to do and how to get results the fastest, simplest, and easiest way possible. Let's face it, darlings. Who has time for complicated things, right?

I hope this book will give you some guidance and confidence in building and scaling your business by focusing on what's important to you and your clients, instead of the glitter that the market is telling you that you need. Choose the methods that work the best for you and practice them every day. You'll start to see results. At the end of this book, I shared my five steps on how you can quickly make money in your business.

Here's to your success and dreams of making a positive impact on society!

Best wishes,

Izdihar

Money Makers

Dr. Izdihar Jamil, Ph.D.

"Keep things simple and the money will follow."

— Dr. Izdihar Jamil

The Market

"You can only sell what the market wants."

— Dr. Izdihar Jamil

I remember when I first wanted to create my online course, my goal was to help moms and women to save money. I thought it was going to be an amazing experience. I believe that this is exactly what moms want because a lot of families are struggling to save money due to the high expenses. I thought I had hit a golden niche, and I was going to be rich very soon.

So when I was in Montreal, Canada, at a conference, I started to design the course. I spent weeks and months perfecting it down to the last word. I wanted it to be flawless before I showed it to the world.

Then one day, after hours and hours of work, the course was finally ready, and I decided, *"OK, I'm going to sell it now! I can't wait to be rich."*

Or so I thought. I used my social media platform to talk about the course, about its importance, my vision, the benefits, and how it can help moms to save money.

People were reaching out to talk to me about my course. I was taking a step toward success, and I was excited!

The Reality

Guess how many of the courses I sold. Here's the reality. I sold *zero*. Yes, you heard me right. I sold *zero*. Nobody bought the course, and I was left completely mind-boggled. How could this be? I was upset, frustrated, and disappointed. I started to blame the world, saying that the problem is in them and not in the course I worked so hard to create.

At one point, I had a conversation with the moms where they told me that they were having a hard time managing their money. Expenses were getting higher and higher, and it was hard for them to save money. Often they would use their credit card to float to the next month. This caused them to incur some debts that were piling up. So I knew there was a need for my course to help them.

So where did I go wrong? The better question would be: *what did I miss?* Then it occurred to me that all this while I was thinking about what tools my clients should have instead of what they truly needed or desired. I was putting the focus on “me” versus “them”.

It’s All About Them

Reality is that it’s not about me. Business is about them - my clients. It's about what the market wants - you can only sell what the market wants. It’s about figuring out what’s important to them and how you can solve their problems.

It’s all about the market.

So with this understanding that it’s all about the market, I took myself out of the equation - about what I want, what I think they need - and started to replay the conversations that I had with my potential clients. I looked for clues and feedback; this time, I really listened to *them*.

In my reflection, I discovered that there were two things that were unappealing in my offer. The first was the length of my course. The second was the price point.

(If you want to find out more about my story, you can go check out my book *13 Key Strategies To Make Money Fast In Business*. It’s available on *Amazon*.)

The Tweaking

The moms were stressed out and frustrated because expenses were getting higher. They felt that the money was slipping away from their pockets and there’s nothing they could do to be in control. As I mentioned earlier, some of them were even piling up debt just to float their families ahead.

Basically, they were almost at a flat-line and were spiraling down with their finances. Naturally, my 10-week course wasn't going to cut it. Why? Because they needed to see the results now, not in 10 weeks.

Upon that realization, I decided to shorten my course. From 10 weeks, I shifted it to seven days. That's the first point based on the feedback that I tweaked. The second problem was the price point. The moms were already pretty much stretched out, so for them to spend thousands of dollars on a course would counteract their logic. They would like to pay off their debt or cover their expenses rather than spending thousands on a course.

So, from thousands of dollars, I shifted the amount to $497 to make it easy and affordable for them. What I was looking for was a way in. Once they had solidified their finances and built their trust in me, I could easily upsell them to my higher services and products should they want to continue working with me.

Now, after the tweaking, I was offering the moms and women to control their expenses and start saving money within seven days for just $497. So even if they saved $100 a month, it wouldn't take them more than five months to make all their money back from my course. After that, it would just be profit for them.

After tweaking my offer, it was time to test my new offer by pre-selling the course.

Pre-Selling

What I did before was that I developed the whole course before I started to sell it. As you know, it didn't turn out great because nobody bought the course, and it cost me my time and energy. This time, I wanted to do things differently. I wanted to see if the market was "biting" on this offer first before I started working on the course. If there would be a demand and commitment, I could easily create the course. If there wasn't, I could change my offers quickly with minimal time, money, and energy spent. How? Because I was pre-selling my idea instead of selling a finished program.

So I tested the offer out and started to pre-sell the course. I tested out my 7-day course for $497. I made my message sharper based on the feedback. I focused on mentioning how my course could help women save money with consistency and predictability every month. I put posts and videos on my social media. I reached out to friends and the people in my network.

And that's my magic formula!

And guess what? It's a *Yes*. People started purchasing the course. I sold my course multiple times over. I finally had money in the bank!

The transition from *zero* to *Yes* came by giving the market exactly what they needed. That's the magic formula. It isn't about you. It's about giving the market exactly what they want because you can only sell what the market wants.

The Magic Conversion Formula

So here's the magic conversion formula. Take yourself out of the equation for a moment and look at what it is that your market truly wants. Then match your skills with the challenges in your market and offer them exactly what they want. The key here is offering a product or service that fits their needs accurately. Imagine a puzzle fitting perfectly into its slots - that's when the magic of conversion will happen. It's one of the best formulae that I've discovered in making money without having to run expensive ads or having a big following.

The truth is that you don't need to run expensive ads or have a big following to make money in your business. Even if you run paid advertising, but you don't know what the audience wants, you're not going to make any conversion from that. All it takes is for you to master the magic formula - offering the market exactly what they want so that it's a perfect fit between you and them.

Remember to always listen to the feedback that you receive and continuously tweak your offer until you find your own magic formula. Your market's feedback is your biggest key to understanding what they desire. People don't care about you. They care about themselves. Your job is to find out how you can help them and nail the perfect solution for them. You may not get a conversion right away, but the point is for you to focus on getting better and better by listening to the feedback of your audience and tweaking things that will be the best fit for them.

Another piece of advice: pre-sell your idea to test it in the market without developing the whole product first. You can tweak things really fast with an idea. That's how you can dynamically shift with your market.

Power Summary

Fill in the blanks and answer the questions.

1. What is my magic formula that I shared in my story?
2. Before launching your product, I mentioned you need to test your idea by _______________.
3. You can only sell what the ________________ wants.

Key Actions

Here are some actions that you can take to help you move forward.

1. Reflect on your market. Write 1 common thing that you've noticed.
2. Incorporate that common thing in your message.
3. Then test it out on your social media.

To access the action plan and materials for this chapter, go to:

https://www.izdiharjamil.com/resources

"You can only sell what the market wants."

— Dr. Izdihar Jamil

All Eyes Are On You

"You have to demand the attention of your tribe. Imagine if your word would be on the front cover of Forbes *magazine. What would you say?"*

— Dr. Izdihar Jamil

Can You See Me?

When I was doing my leadership program, one of the things that I had to do as part of my commitment was to assist at events. One day, I was helping out at one of the events, and I was assigned to work at the registration desk. My job was simple. When people came in, I would help them to fill in the registration cards and give them their name tags.

As I didn't like to be in the spotlight, I was nervous and scared. I was the kind of person who just wanted to help out behind the scenes because I was really shy. But there I was at the front, the first person that the guests would see when they came in.

However, when the program began and people started to pour in, I noticed something strange. Even though I was physically there, people were getting registered with the person on my right or to the person on my left, and somehow they skipped me. Mostly, I felt like I wasn't even there. I asked myself, *Why aren't people registering with me? I'm right in front of them.* One of the things that I needed to do as part of my program was to calculate the number of people who registered with me, in order to see my effectiveness. And as it turned out, I wasn't that effective at all.

After the event, I talked to a friend of mine. I shared with her how puzzled I was about nobody wanting me to help them with their registration process. She asked me, "Did you make yourself invisible, so that you're not seen?"

"What do you mean?" I asked her. She explained that sometimes you can play a hiding game because you don't want to be seen and just want to be in the background. I was surprised that she brought that up because it was true. I was too shy to be seen. I didn't believe that I was good enough. So when people came in, it was as if I had an invisibility cape on and they naturally moved to my right or left because I didn't make myself visible enough for them to be pulled toward me.

The Shift

After that disappointing event, I talked to myself. OK, this is not working. It's going to mess up my stats in this program. So I need to change things.

I began my preparations for the next event. I worked on shifting my mindset and created a game with myself to help me through the program. This time, I wanted to be in the spotlight and to shine my brightest. I wanted everybody to notice me and register with me for the event.

I remember changing everything about myself—my clothing, my smile, and my postures. I wore nice and vibrant clothes. I stood straighter with my head high and moved toward the front. And when the guests came in, I looked at them, made eye contact, and smiled. I showed them that I was excited to see them. I worked on myself to be warm, inviting, and eye-catching. I was done playing behind the scenes.

And that was when the shift started to happen. Guess who people were lining up to register with? Me! Not with the person on my right nor with the person on my left. They lined up in front of me, and I expressed how super excited I was to be helping them with their registration process. It was all about saying hello, helping them fill in the details on their guest cards, and giving them their name badge. But it was one of the best things in the world for me, and I was really enjoying it.

That kind of creativity and energy is infectious because more and more people wanted to register with me. It went to a point that my colleagues began to ask me, "Why are they all registering with you?"

"Because I'm awesome." I replied. Yes, you need to give some credit to yourself, too.

Be Visible and Irresistible

Through this experience, I learned that being visible and demanding people's attention is one of the keys to my business success. It is how I am able to attract amazing clients on social media. They get my vibe and energy, and they like it. They can't resist my warm connection, as well as my happy and nurturing values. That's how I made myself visible, so that I'm seen all the time.

Before, I was lost within thousands of other coaches and consultants. Now, *I stand out because I choose to own the spotlight*. I choose to be the *Queen* of my QUEENDOM.

There are thousands and thousands of coaches and consultants that are using social media to get clients. The question is, how are they going to see you if you're playing the invisible game? It's like you're there, but you're not there. Just like I was physically there at the registration desk, but people couldn't see me. So they passed by me to go to my other colleagues.

If you want to make money without ads, without spending thousands, or without having thousands of followers, you have to be highly visible and irresistible, so that people can see you and be attracted to you. For example, when you post some text or video on social media, you've got to create something impressive so that it hits the platform with a bang, and so that all eyes are on you.

Imagine if your post or video would be on the front cover of *Forbes* magazine, one of the most iconic brands. What would you say that would be so impactful? Would you put a picture of a flower? Or say something valuable that will be irresistible to people and captivate your audience.

Exactly! You would say something big and meaningful that will hopefully have an impact on your audience for years to come.

Let me say it again. When you post on social media, or do a presentation video, make sure that you demand your audience's attention.

All eyes are on you.

All eyes are on you and no one else.

Breaking the Pattern

So whether you use beautiful colors, bold letters, classic patterns, or emoji, make sure to add a "hook" in your statement that speaks directly to your audience. You can also be using pretty, clear, sharp, and focused images of yourself so that you're directing their eyes toward your captivating personality. It's like when everybody is wearing black and you walk in, being the only one wearing red.

Who are people going to look at?

That's right. They are going to be looking at you, because you have something that excites them. You're different. They are curious about you. They are intrigued by you and what you have to offer because you're interrupting the normal pattern.

Imagine when you put up a post or video on social media. You're showing up with the brightest smile, wearing beautiful clothes, and have eye-catching taglines. You're setting a certain vibe and energy that is attracting a particular audience. Instead of writing a hard to read message, you write 2-3 impactful and eye-catching headlines.

You're keeping things simple yet at the same time demanding your audience's attention through your use of powerful images and words that are connecting you with them. You're sending out a positive vibe, and you are shining your brightest. That's what you need to do to be visible.

So who is your audience going to choose? Someone who's hiding behind the scene? No.

They'll be choosing you.

Here's an example. A podcast host reached out to me on social media and wanted to interview me for her podcast show. Why? Because every time she would check her social media, she saw me posting about my work, methods, my clients' successes, my impressive results, and my values. All of that stood out amongst other posts, and it intrigued her.

She said, "I gotta reach out to this lady!"

How cool is that! Having people that are constantly reaching out to you because they see you frequently on social media and find you impressive. Following that we created a collaboration after our conversation because we found out that we could support each other in moving forward with our business.

The general rule of marketing is that they need to see you between 15-20 times before they buy into your brand. That's why big companies and businesses run their advertisements over and over again over a period of time to create the trust and credibility factors with their audience. That's why showing up consistently and frequently will help boost your visibility and bring you into the spotlight.

Everyday Posting

To be visible and to grab the attention of the world, you need to post on social media every day.

Why?

Because when you post on a social media platform every day, the algorithm recognizes you. The algorithm favors you because its job is to collect data. The more data that it has on you, the more importance it will give to your account, and it will boost up your posts and videos. If you commit to posting frequently, the algorithm is going to increase the reach of your post, which will increase your audience. Why? Again, because it thinks that you're someone important. A few of the feedback that I commonly receive from people are: "You're always at the top of my newsfeed." and "I see you on social media all the time!" This happens because I stay active and engage on a daily basis.

Just ask yourself this question: Would your audience rather choose someone who rarely shows up or someone who shows up every day?

Of course, they'll choose someone who shows up every day. Because that gives them assurance that the person they're following is committed, reliable, and serious about their work.

So make yourself visible and demand their attention. Remember, all eyes are on you. Figure out how you can tweak things so that you can stand out amongst thousands of influencers on social media.

Ask yourself, how can you make them choose you, just owning your authenticity and individuality? How can you make them focus on you? A few tips: You can do simple things like, say something outrageous or controversial, wear a nice dress, use bold colors or patterns, or say something significant. Then repeat it every day, and you will start to see results.

Power Summary

Let's recap the key points in this chapter. Fill in the blanks and answer the questions.

1. Fill in the blank. All Eyes _____________.
2. Declare out loud: I am the Queen of my Queendom and I am ready to be in the spotlight.

3. How often do you need to show up on social media to be highly visible?

Key Actions

Here is your one action that can help you to get started with your success.

1. Put a post on social media today with the best picture of you. Add 2-3 lines and make that impactful.
2. Repeat it every day for 30 days.

To access the action plan and materials for this chapter, go to:

https://www.izdiharjamil.com/resources

Leveraging Social Media

"Social media is a great tool to attract thousands of clients around the world within seconds of you posting!"

— Dr. Izdihar Jamil

Leveraging social media is one of the fastest ways that you can grow your business without paying for expensive advertisements. Just by posting one post or video, your message can reach out to thousands of people around the world within seconds. It's accessible to everybody and best of all, it's free. Social media is the #1 tool that I use to attract potential clients and then convert them into paid clients.

If you want your business to grow but you haven't opened up your social media account, you need to do it now. Which social media account should you have? My answer would be all of them - *Facebook, Instagram, LinkedIn*, and *Twitter*. Why? Because each platform has its particular purpose and will attract certain clients.

Purpose of Social Media

Here is a quick breakdown of the purpose of different social media platforms based on my interaction with thousands of entrepreneurs and business owners. You can get started with one or two platforms, but it's best for you to be visible on the majority of them. This will allow your audience to find and connect with you easily.

- ***Facebook***: For leisure and social activities. It's where people come to hang out and chill. It has a more relaxed environment as compared to other platforms, a place where you can connect to people and share stories about your success, methods, wisdom, offers, etc.

- ***LinkedIn***: For business and professional use. It's where people come to use their network. *LinkedIn* has the ability to narrow down your target audience, which makes it easier for you to pinpoint your ideal clients and get in touch with them.
- ***Instagram***: *Instagram* features influencers and lifestyles of different people. This is the place where influencers hang out. They often have a tribe of people following them. One thing to note about *Instagram* is that the usage of stunning and aesthetic pictures and creative videos play a big role in building your audience.
- ***Twitter***: It exhibits the latest arguments on politics, society, and journalism. This is where most of the editors, journalists, and media people hang out. So if you want to connect with editors, journalists, and producers, this is the place to be.

In general, there are three types of activities that you can do on social media - posting, story, and a Live video. Posting is when you post on social media with your picture or text. You can write a long or a short post.

Story is the concise version of your post, often with just one picture and 1-2 short lines of text. A Live video is, as the term suggests, when you do a video live on social media. Your audiences are able to interact with you while you are doing a live video, and you can also invite a guest to join you.

Making Money on Social Media

Non-entrepreneurs use social media to share their life with the public. The content of the posts and videos present fun, leisure, and light-hearted content. While on the other hand, entrepreneurs and business owners use social media to attract clients and make money from it. Hence, there is a particular way of writing your posts or making your videos that will turn your followers into paid clients.

The best formula that I've discovered and I personally use to attract and convert clients on social media is the 2/3 rule. 2/3 of your content on social media should be about your business, success, transformations you created, results of your experiences with your clients.

1/3 of your content can be about your personal life. You want to mix it with the professional stuff so that your audience can connect with you on a personal level, too. In my business, on Mondays to Fridays, my content is geared toward attracting clients, featuring my services and offers, engagement-type interaction, advice, and my success stories. On the weekends, I usually share my personal life, like my baking skills, family activities, and my life as a mom. Often, personal stories can also be part of your business brand.

Your ONE purpose on Social Media

So when you post or do a video on social media, it should have one purpose and one purpose only, to attract and convert clients. That's why your posts on social media are so valuable. It's not enough to upload a picture of a flower or your pet, unless you know how to convert it into money in the bank. Again, think about your post like it's going to be on the front cover of *Forbes* magazine. What would be so impactful and significant that is worthy of your post?

Ask yourself the following questions when you're leveraging social media.

1. Am I attracting the right clients?
2. Am I speaking their language?
3. Am I delivering what they want?
4. What will make them say Yes to me?
5. What will make them reach out to me?

Make your posts and videos simple and yet impactful with just a few lines. People don't have the time to read an essay. Think of it this way, if you can only write just one line, what would it be? Write something that would strip down all the "fluff" and help you focus on making the point. In other words, what you have to say is so precious that just one line is all it takes to make an impact.

Mastering the arts of writing impactful 2-3 lines in your social media will also serve to your advantage. Here's the thing. When you post, people will only see the first 2-3 lines before they click on more. If your important message is in line 20, chances are your audience is not going to get it. Hence, you'll lose out on the opportunity to convert them. So be smart when crafting your message.

Majority of social media now favors the story feature. Story is just a snapshot or the short version of your post. You can only post your picture and a very, very short message on a story. Stories are usually visible for 24 hours and are placed on the top of any social media platform. In other words, social media platforms are now giving priority to stories versus videos or posting. So again, to utilize the story feature, you have to nail down your message in 2-3 effective lines.

If you can only write one line, and that one line makes you $1000 dollars or more, what would you say?

Another important thing is to have a call to action in your social media content. You want to lead. You want to direct your audience to take particular action. That is how you turn your audience from followers to paid clients - by guiding them to take action on your offers. A call to action can be something simple such as “Say Yes if you’re interested” or “Drop me an emoji if you want more info".

Posting Formula

Here are some posting formulas on social media that I have personally tested and taught my clients. They are very effective in attracting clients to your account and posts. When you have mastered this formula, you can grow your business and make money without paying for advertisements or having a big following. My clients and I have made a lot of money by using these posting formulae.

#1 The Love Formula

Example:

Would you love to __________?
(Mention result/transformation/offer in the blank)

Say “YES” and I’ll share my secrets.

The first line in the example is “Would you love to _________?”

In the blank, you would put the result, transformation, or offer that your market wants. This is also a great way for you to test your idea before you develop your product to see if this is something that will intrigue your audience.

The second line is *“Say YES and I’ll share my secrets.”*

It is a form of a call to action. It’s important that you encourage them to take a particular action if they're interested in your offer. Once they respond, you can schedule a call or meeting with them, invite them to watch your webinar, or direct them to the next step in your process.

Based on testing, the formula has a higher conversion when you put a number in. It gives your audience something tangible that they can measure. Of course, you can't put a number for everything, but when possible, do include a number to increase your conversion.

Examples:

Would you love to increase your income in 30 days?

Drop me a "$" and I'll send you my secrets.

Would you love to be a Bestselling Author in 90 days?

Say "YES"! I've got something exciting for you.

Would you love to lose 10lb in 7 days?

Comment "10" and I'll share my methods.

#2 The Call Out Formula

Examples:

Who's an Entrepreneur?

Drop me an emoji. Let's connect!

The purpose of this formula is to call out to your particular niche. Straight away in the first line, "*Who's an Entrepreneur?*" is calling out to all the entrepreneurs who view your post. The second line "*Drop me an emoji. Let's connect!*" is a call to action to encourage your viewers.

Examples:

Who's an Author?
Say , "ME".

Who's a Fitness Coach?
Drop me an emoji.

Who's a Business Owner?
Comment, "I am".

Attracting clients on social media is as simple as that. Of course, there are many more formulas like these that you can use to engage people. In my course *The Client Conversion System*, I teach my clients the variation of the formulae and how to use them. Here's the thing, you don't need to know a million formulae. You just need to know a few and master them so well that they convert every time you put them out to use.

Let's say you put out either the Love or the Call Out formula once a week and 50 people respond. Out of the 50, 5 become your paid clients at $2K each. So in a week you can make $10K by using that one formula alone. Even if only 1 person responded and you convert that person at $2K, you'll still be making $2K that week. You see, it's that easy to attract and convert using a simple formula.

In other words, high engagements don't mean much if you're not able to convert. Ideally, you want to convert every person who responds to your offer. Some of them may not be your ideal clients. Regardless, even converting one potential client is a success in my book.

30-Day Challenge

When I first got started, I challenged myself to post and do a video every day for 30 days. Why? Because I wanted to increase my reach and win my audience's confidence fast. It's been scientifically proven that human beings need 30 days to install a new habit. I wanted to get more clients, so I needed to leverage more on social media and be visible. The 30-day challenge helped me to stay focused on building my business.

My audience and confidence grew rapidly. People were starting to notice me. And now it has become part of my habit. I have become really good at posting on social media to attract clients. Each post that I do is worth at least $1000 because I'm able to convert clients. Now, posting on social media has become really easy and fast for me because I have practiced that muscle.

Power Summary

Let's recap on the key points from this chapter. Fill in the blanks and answer the questions.

1. What are the two formulas that I use to attract clients?
2. What is the one purpose of social media for entrepreneurs?
3. You can lead by placing a call to __________ line in your post.

Key Actions

Here are your actions to help you move forward:

1. Choose either the Love or Call Out formula.
2. Craft your message based on the formula that you chose.
3. Post it on your social media.
4. When people respond, lead them to the next step of your process, for example, a call.

To access the action plan and materials for this chapter, go to:

https://www.izdiharjamil.com/resources

"Social media is a great tool to attract thousands of clients around the world within seconds of you posting!"

— Dr. Izdihar Jamil

The ABC Rule

"Attract - Book - Convert is the simplest client conversion system that you need to remember."

— Dr. Izdihar

My client conversion system is really simple. It's just ABC. Attract - Book - Convert. I like to keep things simple and avoid the complicated. If anything is complicated, I'm going to run away from it the first chance I get.

So I advise you to just keep it simple as well. ABC, that's the only client conversion system that I use. That's the method I use to teach my clients how to make money in the business. Attract, Book, and Convert. In the previous chapter, I discussed using social media as a tool to attract clients, because social media is a fantastic tool that is accessible to almost everybody.

Has social media been helpful in attracting your ideal clients to you? We discussed in the previous chapter on how you can do that, and in this chapter, I'll share with you another important and helpful rule, the ABC rule.

People Buy People

Now, what we are using here is value-based marketing and attraction-based marketing. We're not using product-based marketing. There's a difference between value-based marketing and attraction-based marketing versus product-based marketing. Product based markets run on products.

You're promoting a product, such as your health supplements, beauty products, and essential oils. But what you should be doing is attracting people to you, using your values, your principles, and your essence.

Imagine you as the shining light that attracts these amazing people to you who are in alignment with the principles, with your values, in alignment with your services and with your vision. You've got to think of yourself as a magnetic attraction machine.

People buy people. If you're selling a product by focusing on the product, it's going to be hard for people to connect with you. People are only interested in buying the products that others have tried and have grown to like and admire. People buy people, not just products.

So first, they would check out the person representing the product if they're interested. The things that the potential clients look for are trust factor, having a relationship, forming a connection with the person, and then buying into their products and services. So attraction is one of the main tools.

For example, when you put a post on social media, you'll need to attract the clients to your values, attract them to your personality, success, and your vision. I'll give you an example, one which really worked for me. One of the things that I offer is to help women to be a best-selling author in 90 days.

Invite Them to the Results

So what I offer them and attract them to is positioning as a go-to expert by being a best-selling author, because there's authority and credibility that comes with it. When I post, I'm attracting those people who want to write a book or who want to be a bestselling author. I could write something like, *Who's got 'Write a Book' in the bucket list this year?*

You want to attract them to your vision, results, services, and offer. Naturally, people who respond to your post would be the people who are interested in what you have to offer, in my example, those who want to write a book or be an author. Remember to always lead them somewhere. You want to lead them somewhere, not just leave them hanging.

You could also attract them to your success, personality, journey, and principles. For example, when I was nominated to be in the Who's Who in America or when I was featured on Fox TV, I shared about my success, journey, and excitement. This creates credibility and trust factor with the audience, which is the key in converting them. People want to work with people that they trust.

Call to Action

A call to action is simply an invitation for people to take action. You don't need to put a call to action in all your posts because then it becomes robotic. Include a call to action on messages that you want them to take some action. If you're sharing a personal story or reflection, you may not need to add a call to action.

A call to action can be as simple as asking your audience to post a heart emoji or asking people to comment "Yes" on your post. You can choose the kind of call to action according to the theme of your post or video. A call to action is also a great way to build the bridge between you and your audience even if it's just asking them to say "Hello".

It's something like this. You have people here on your left who have been following you, and on your right you have you. But there's a prominent gap between the left and the right, that is, there is a gap between you and them. If you're wondering why you haven't got any clients from your social media, now you know- there is a gap! And the question is, how can you create a bridge to fix the gap and connect the two ends with each other? How can you cross over the bridge between you and them?

That's where the call to action comes in. A call to action is what will bridge the gap between you and them. Once your audience responds to your invitation, we can now go to the next step - booking them into a call with you.

Booking

We've attracted them to you by building a bridge between you and them, and to build a bridge, you lead them with a call to action. For example, *Say "Yes" if you're interested in it. If you want more information, say Hello.*

This way, you'll build a bridge and you'll be leading them somewhere.

And when they respond to your call to action by saying "Yes" or dropping a heart or doing whatever it is the call to action invited them to do, you can now personally send them a message. Send them a message saying hi. Greet them. Say, *Hello. Thank you for responding to my post. Would you be interested in finding out more about this?*

Then check in with them again. So you want to make sure that when they say Yes, they are giving you the permission to contact them, and that you're able to invite them to check out your offer. You can also offer more information. What personally works for me is either to offer to have a call with them or invite them to come to my virtual events.

For example, if they are interested to learn how to be the #1 go-to expert in their field and get in the media, *Forbes*, TV, magazine, and *TED*, I would personally send them an invitation to my "Top Authority Activation Virtual Retreat".

You can find out more about my virtual retreat here:

https://www.izdiharjamil.com/fast-authority

And that's the booking part. Booking means you lead them somewhere, whether it's a call, your free training, e-book, retreats, etc. The key is leading them to a specific process or result that you want to achieve.

Direct Message

Part of the attraction process is also for you to be engaging directly with your audience. If you're short on time, you can always hire a virtual assistant to do this as long as you've given them clear directions on the process.

With direct messaging, you basically send them a personal message with the intention of creating a connection or offering something of value to them. There are many simple things you can begin with. You can say things like,

Hi, Sarah, quick question. Would you love some tips on how to be featured on TV and magazines?

And in the end, sign your name.

If you want to test out several messaging or direct message, which we call messenger commerce, the cool part is that you can send them a message at any point. The biggest myths people have is playing the "waiting game", i.e. I can only message that person when she/he responds back to me. I would always recommend that you take the initiative or the first step in building that connection.

For all you know, people could be shy to reach out to you. So when you take the initiative to reach out to them, they could get excited and this is when you open the doors of communication.

All you have to do in the first instance is drop them a quick and simple message. For example, you can say,

Hi Amanda,
You're doing amazing work (compliment!). Would you love some tips on how to get on the media and Forbes*?*

Izdihar

This is to me a seemingly simple message that you can use, just two simple lines. Quick tip: Don't bombard people with links, especially in the first message. Remember to say hello. Keep it simple because a confused mind never buys. If you write like 20 lines, people are going to get confused. They're not going to be interested.

So that's the attraction and booking part. Next, we're going to be moving on to the converting part of the formula.

The Conversion

The conversion part is basically the exchange of money and transactions between you and your clients. Most people know this as the sales call, where you offer them the opportunity to work with you and you seal the deal when they make the payment in exchange for your products or services. There can be times when you don't need to chat with them, but you can still convert them simply by emailing or messaging them. Regardless, the key here is the conversion—from followers to paid clients.

I'll be talking more about conversion and sales calls in my coming chapter on sales. But now that you've attracted them to you, you've built the bridge between you and them, you've got them in on a call with you. Now here's the key thing about conversion that many people forget. Do you remember what I told you in Chapter 1, that it's all about the market?

The YES comes when you're able to solve the problems for them, not when you try to sell your own agenda. That's all you've got to think about, bringing value to them by solving their problems. Once they are attracted to your offer, just ask if they would be interested in working with you to achieve the results that you've discussed.

When they say YES, all you have to do is direct them to the payment methods for the money to flow into your bank account. For the YES to happen, remember that your potential clients have to be ready mentally, financially, and physically. Sometimes the timing is off. Sometimes they are not ready yet to invest due to other commitments.

Rejection is inevitable. What's important for you to understand is that your ideal clients that are committed to their own success and find that your offer is valuable will say YES to you. Those who don't, it just means that they are not a good fit for you at the moment. It is possible that they will come back to you at some point should they feel the alignment with you.

There are millions of clients for you out there who are just waiting for you. Those are the people that you want to serve.

So that's it. The ABC Rule: Attract, Book, Convert.

Power Summary

Fill in the blanks and answer the questions.

1. For attraction-based marketing, you need to attract people to ______________.
2. There is a gap between you and them. How do you build a bridge to close the gap?
3. When does the conversion happen?

Key Actions

Here are the actions that will help you keep moving forward.

1. Send 10 people a simple 2-line message.
2. When they respond, invite them to have a call with you.
3. Convert them or offer them the opportunity to work with you if you feel that you're a good fit for each other.

To access the action plan and materials for this chapter, go to:

https://www.izdiharjamil.com/resources

Authority

"Authority leads to trust and conversion."

— Dr. Izdihar Jamil

If you want to make money in your business, the fastest way possible without ads is to position yourself as the top authority in your field. I'm not talking about being just an authority. I'm talking about being the top 1% authority in your field. Why do you want to be at the top? Because that's where all the money is and that's where the best clients are.

Just like when you want to go and see a doctor, would you go to a doggy doctor or the best doctor in the area? Absolutely, you'll go to the best doctor even if you have to pay a little more. It's the same principle in business. Clients only want to work with the best in the industry. The top people in any industry are the ones who make the most money.

The good thing about being an authority is that it's buildable and doable. When I started my entrepreneurial journey, I was a computer scientist who wanted to work from home, so I can take care of my family. I was totally unknown in the business world. Yet, within just a few short years, I have positioned myself as the #1 go-to media expert. My work has been recognized by *Forbes*, *TED*, *Fox TV*, magazines, media, and influencers around the world.

In this chapter, I'm going to share with you simple methods that you can use—that I and my clients have personally used—to position yourself as a top authority.

Credibility

Imagine this. When your ideal clients do research on you, on one hand, they have Sarah, who's a self-proclaimed coach or entrepreneur just like you. And they have you on the other hand, but you come with authority endorsements from globally trusted organizations. For example, you're a #1 bestselling author. *Forbes* has featured you, and you've been interviewed by the high-profile podcasts. You've also been featured on TV and in magazines. So which one between Sarah and you are your ideal clients going to choose?

You!

That's right, because you have credibility and authority. You have been endorsed by globally trusted organizations that say: *Yes, I'm endorsing this person. She is an expert.*

So it means that you are, because globally trusted organizations are extending their trust factor to you by featuring or endorsing you on their platforms. You now have that trust factor with you. For example, when *Forbes*, one of the most iconic brands in the world features you, it means that they are recognizing you as the top of the pack. *Forbes* has featured billionaires like presidents and influential leaders.

When you're on *Forbes*, you're instantly a celebrity due to the prestigious associations. And that will make it easy for people to trust you, makes it really easy for you to sell your brand with ease. Now the only thing left for you to do is figure out if you're a good match with that person, if you can help them, and if they are the right fit for you and your business.

I remember when I first started; I had to work extremely hard to convince people that I'm an expert. So I know when it comes to my expertise, I was exhausted because I spent so much time and energy convincing people. But when you have this globally recognized brand endorsing you, saying, *Yes, I'm approving this person*, it's so much easier for the clients to have that trust-trigger with you.

You can go straight to the point with your solution or expertise because you've already got the credibility factor and the authority factor. In other words, your brand sells itself and that's so much easier than having to convince people that you're an expert. Now, you just are!

How to Achieve Credibility and Authority

One of the first things that you can do to be an authority is to write a book. Not just any book, but a bestselling book, just like what I'm doing now. If possible, go all the way to the #1 international bestselling status. I myself am really blessed that my clients and I are #1 international bestselling authors. We have specific methods and strategies to make it into bestseller status.

If writing a book is something you're interested in, you can go and check out my website www.izdiharjamil.com/resources. You'll find an idea-to-book mini planner to start planning for your book. My team and I are also offering a FREE 1:1 consultation to help you plan your book and authority building.

When you're a published author and you're holding a book that you've written with your name on the front cover, the mindset of your audience is that you're automatically an expert. The audience has been trained by legendary figures like Jack Canfield, Napoleon Hill, and Oprah, who have written books, that by being an author you're instantly an authority.

You don't have to do a lot of convincing. You don't have to do a lot of advertising. The mindset of people is that when you have a book, especially if you have a #1 bestselling book, you're a top authority. That's how people think, and smart people like you know how to leverage that to your advantage.

Let me ask you this, how many books have you bought this year alone? Quite a few, right? And what made you buy that book? Here are my guesses: number one, because you wanted to solve your problems and the book offers an idea about how you can do that. And number two, a book is an easy investment to learn new things and techniques as compared to spending thousands to attend a seminar or a course. A book is usually around 10 to 20 dollars, so it's an easy investment for anybody to buy into your brand.

So what happens to me is that people from my audience or followers would buy my book because they like an idea that I shared that could help solve their problems. Once they read it, they love the book and my story. They love my idea, and then they get in touch with me either via email or social media.

When I feel that we are a good fit for one another, I invite them to have a conversation with me so I can find out more about them and vice versa. Often, that conversation will lead to a commitment and a contract as we choose to work together on a particular project. When that happens, there is an exchange of money and services between my clients and me. And as you can see, it all starts with a book, and that's one of the ways that you can create money in the bank.

Writing a Book

Now, there are a few things that you want to remember when you're writing a book.

You're not going to get rich just by selling books, because you'll be getting a few dollars per book that you sell. I have calculated that for me to make $10,000 a month; I have to sell around 50,000 books per month. Now that's a lot of books and energy that you have to sell to make $10,000 a month.

So what's the secret to making money through books?

The secret to growing your income and business is to leverage your book. For example, you could use that book as a lead magnet to attract amazing clients to you. What I mean by a lead magnet is that it is something that you offer as a result of people doing something. The classic example is you offer them your book when they sign up to your mailing list or webinar. When they read your book and further solidify your trust and credibility factors with them, they are more likely to reach out to you to enquire about your services. For example, if your book can get 10 clients who are paying around $5000 each. That's really $50,000 for you just from your book.

I remember one of the first personal development books that I purchased was T. Harv Eker's *Secrets of the Millionaire Mind*. In his book, he talked about his seminar. Guess what? I ended up going to his seminar and further invested in his programs! So a book is really your brochure about your business and the key to making money without spending thousands of dollars on advertising.

The way I see it, a book is an act of service to leave your parting wisdom to the world. When you play it right, a book is also a money-making tool to help you get amazing clients and other opportunities. This has worked for me and has worked for many of my clients. For example, my client, Jessica, used her book as a way to make $25,000 in her business just from that one method that she taught in her book. How cool is that!

The Process of Writing a Book

To write a book, there are a few steps that you want to follow. I teach these methods in my Top Authority Activation Virtual Retreat. You are welcome to join me and to learn in a safe and intimate environment. It's a free retreat for women at https://www.izdiharjamil.com/fast-authority.

First, you need to have a topic, an idea, or a theme that your audience wants. Remember what I said earlier. It's all about the market. You can only sell what the market wants. So you have to come up with a book idea that's going to help solve the problems of the people that you are serving. Be as specific as possible because when you try to go broad on your topic, you will help no one because your idea is too generalized.

For example, my client Veronica, who is a doctor in oriental medicine and a licensed acupuncturist, wrote a book called *Unlocking Your Super Life: A Guide to a Healthier and Happier You.* She wanted people to have a healthier life using holistic mind-body-spiritual methods. So she's helping people with their wellness through a very specific method.

Another example, this book, *Money Makers*, is about how entrepreneurs can build and scale their business without spending thousands of dollars on expensive advertising or having a big following. It's also about using organic trust-credibility-authority methods to attract and convert the right clients for your business.

How can you know what the problems are and what to solve?

Here are my guidelines to finding out your topic or idea for your book that can help you solve people's problems:

1. Ask the people in your niche what their biggest problems or challenges are.
2. What's the number one question that you're often asked to solve?
3. What's your expertise or solution that has been proven to help others?
4. Reflect back on your previous conversations. What's the common theme?
5. What's the number one thing that people ask your advice for?

Know that there is an abundance of ideas. Just look at the books that are out on *Amazon* every day. You probably have a few ideas of your own. It's just a matter of putting it in a book format, using the right system with the right team. It's that simple.

If a 6-year-old can do it, so can you!

Even my daughter, Princess Munchkin, wrote a book when she was 6 years old!

Yes, you heard me, a 6-year-old girl wrote a book.

My daughter is in elementary school. She's learning to read and write, but she had this idea. You see, my daughter loves ponies, and she wants to buy her own ponies. So I said, *OK, but you have to make some money because ponies are expensive.* So we hashed out some ideas on how she can make money and one of her ideas is for her to write a book. She saw me writing several books, and that gave her the inspiration to go for it.

Be mindful that this is a 6-year-old writing a book, so there's nothing complicated. Her idea is simple—she loves ponies. In her storytelling, she shared her love of ponies, her experience riding her first pony, and her dream of owning a pony of her own. It couldn't get any simpler than that, right? That's how the book was called *The Girl Who Loves Ponies*. You can go and check it out on *Amazon*.

Now you have to understand that my daughter doesn't know the whole book publishing process. Truth is, she doesn't need to know the whole thing. All she has is an idea and how to weave it into a story. Children are amazing storytellers and their ability to dream is amazing. As adults, we have forgotten those skills because we are so caught up with reality. All I had to do was to encourage her imagination and storytelling skills.

Because part of my work is helping female entrepreneurs to publish books and be a bestselling author, I already have the team and the skillset to help my daughter to publish and launch her book. We hit #1 bestseller on *Amazon* in America, England, Australia, and Canada.

Testing Your Book Idea

So coming back to the book, all you need is an idea that is going to help solve your niche's problem. That's the whole purpose of being an entrepreneur, solving someone's problem. That's how you make money out of it. And then once you have an idea about it and before you start writing your whole book, I recommend that you test your idea first.

If you don't test it out and you go on to spend months writing your book and on the launch day, nobody wants to buy the book, that's not going to be a pleasant experience. One way to test out your idea is to test it by putting a post on social media.

Hey, I'm thinking about writing a book about ____________ (your topic). What do you think about it?

Then you simply observe the feedback around it.

If nobody is engaging or giving you any feedback, you know that you need to tweak things. It means your idea isn't something that people want at the moment. Or they may want slightly different things. So test out your idea first and see if people are biting it. That's how you become a bestselling author—when you have a lot of people buying your books.

Media

Another way to be an authority is for you to be featured in the media. There are multiple media platforms, and each one has its own purpose and target audience. You need to say yes to any media opportunity that you can get—whether it's with a local or international channel; it doesn't matter. Just say yes to it.

There are top media publications that are just going to be one of the most iconic brands in the world, let's say, *Forbes*, NBC, ABC, Fox TV, etc. So you would want to put a plan on getting those media in your profile.

So how does it work in the media?

You need to understand that the one thing the media wants is content to feed its audience. TV producers, reporters, and journalists are constantly looking for stories and experts to be showcased. For example, one of *Forbes*'s senior writer herself told me that *Forbes* only wants to feature people who are authorities in their fields. *Forbes* is an iconic brand, so to be featured on *Forbes*, you have to be at the top of your game.

3 Ways to Get in the Media

There are three ways for you to get into the media.

First Method

First is by pitching. You can hire a PR company to pitch on your behalf or do it yourself. Some PR companies charge a minimum of $10,000 on a 6-months retainer to do the PR for them.

On the other hand, to do the pitching yourself, you have to know how to do it effectively. You have to know who to send your pitches to, and it's a good idea to have your own perfect pitch template. There are multiple things that you need to have in the template.

One of them is that you need to have a catchy title, as that would be the first thing that the producer, writer, or editor sees. Your title needs to be between 5-7 keywords. You can use the tool at https://www.title-generator.com and enter your keywords and a list of titles will come up. For example, you can key in the word *money* and a list of titles will come up. Feel free to tweak it to fit your topic.

As for the remainder of the ingredients of creating your perfect pitch template, join me on my virtual retreat where I'll be sharing my tips and methods at https://www.izdiharjamil.com/fast-authority.

Second Method

The second method to get in the media is to pay for the advertising spot. You can either hire a PR company to purchase an advertising space in the media or contact the producer directly to do so.

For example, you can contact a TV producer directly to purchase some airtime during one of their shows.

Third Method

The third method is to use your connections to get in front of the right people. At times, people in your network may know someone in the media. You can ask them to hook you up or ask them to arrange a meeting on your behalf. If you do it this way, remember to return the favor that they have shown you.

Speaking

Now, another way for you to be an authority is to be featured in high-profile speaking engagements, such as *TED*. It is one of the most prestigious speaking platforms in the world.

So let's say you get to speak on the *TEDx* stage. Instantly, that creates your authority as one of the best speakers in your area, because not many people can get onto the *TED* platform. This, in turn, will make it easier for you if you want to become a keynote speaker at events or if you want to be paid to train in the corporate world, because of the prestige associated with being a *TEDx* speaker.

You can also get many other speaking engagement opportunities, either virtually or during live events. One of the ways that I get booked on speaking engagements is that I consistently share about my work, my ups, my downs, my success, my journey, and my tips on social media.

When my audience read it, some of them felt inspired by my story and then invited me to speak at their events. Some of them are paid and some of them are not. The main thing is that something good always comes up when I get to speak in front of a group of people.

For example, I share about my book *Yes I Can!* on social media. One of the top podcast hosts saw my story and interviewed me for her podcast. Not only did we have a great time, but it sparked a collaboration between us when she hired me to help her get into the media. Then she referred me to her clients. How cool is that!

Power Summary

Fill in the blanks and answer the questions.

1. The most reliable thing you can do to win credibility is to __________________.
2. You can use a book as a magnet to _________________.
3. How can you find out what problems need to be solved in your niche?
4. Once you have an idea for a book, you first _____________ it in the market.
5. What can you share on social media to help you to get speaking engagements?

Key Actions

Here are a few key actions that will help you move forward.

1. Write down one idea for your book.
2. Put a post or do a video on social media regarding your book idea.
3. Observe the feedback and evaluate whether that is a good idea to move forward with or not.

To access the action plan and materials for this chapter, go to:

https://www.izdiharjamil.com/resources

Authority

"Authority leads to trust and conversion."

— Dr. Izdihar Jamil

The Power of Association

"The quickest way to build trust with a new audience is through the power of association."

— Dr. Izdihar Jamil

Associating yourself to a tribe leader or high-profile influencer is another powerful way to make money without having to pay for advertising or having a big following. What this means is that you're actually putting yourself in front of a well-known leader's audience and network.

Now, that leader or influencer has probably spent a lot of money on their brand, advertising, creating relationships, connections, and the trust factor with their audience.

Rather than spending the time, money, and energy in building that audience, the key here is to hack into that person's audience so that you can offer them an opportunity to solve their problems based on your expertise.

You are tapping into a readily accessible pool of audience. When that tribe leader endorses you and presents you in front of their network, they are extending the trust factor that their audience has with them to you. In a way, they are saying that *"Hey, this person is cool and you can trust them."*

Almost instantly, you have a large audience in front of you that you don't have to work really hard for, just by using the power of association method.

For example, Tony Robbins often invites other experts as guests to his mastery. Tony is one of the top motivational speakers out there, so when he endorses someone to his audience, would you say that his audience would generally trust that person too?

Absolutely!

Because Tony wouldn't be putting people in front of his audience, who may jeopardize his reputation. But only people whom he trusts will be invited as his guests. You can absolutely use this model in your business, too.

I've leveraged this principle multiple times, and it was an amazing experience. I love creating collaborations or joint ventures with people who have the same principles and values as I do.

For example, Connie Benjamin, whom I featured on my Spotlight Female Entrepreneurs Magazine, connected me with the Godmother of Personal Transformation, Marcia Martin. Marcia has trained over 300,000 people around the world, including the industry's top experts, such as Tony Robbins, Jack Canfield, T. Harv Eker, and many more.

I offered to collaborate with her on my book project, *Women Who Lead,* and in return for her to feature me in her podcast or membership. Because I'm a #1 International Bestselling Author and have done multiple book projects, Marcia could see my credibility and authority instantly.

Hence, it made it easy for us to move forward with that collaboration. In the *Women Who Lead* book, Marcia shared her secrets of how she overcame obstacles and built a successful business. You can check out the book *Women Who Lead* on *Amazon.*

Quick tip, before you can even do that, you have to establish yourself as the authority and the go-to expert in your field, because these people, these leaders, are looking for influential figures who're a good fit for their brands. They will not collaborate or endorse just anybody, so you need to make sure that you've built your credibility and authority first.

So if you're someone who's just starting, they'll ask, *OK, how can I trust you? What are the results that you've been producing? Can this person really deliver?*

So what are the ways that you can build your authority?

I've mentioned in the previous chapter that you can use the media, be part of a prestigious speaking platform, or you can be a bestselling author. Set your plan to have multiple forms of authority endorsements as that will elevate your status as an influencer. Once you have a strong foundation for being an authority and an expert in your field, you can present the idea to a tribe leader.

Make It All About Them

Let's break down the steps on how you can approach an influencer or a leader who has a pool audience that is a good fit for you.

Step #1: Research

Do a quick research on them. Check out their social media, websites, and join in their training if possible. Get a feel for them to make sure that your principles and values are aligned with them and vice versa. It's important for both of you to be a good fit for each other.

Step #2: Visible

Start by being visible in front of them on their social media. Comment or share their posts and be genuine about it. When you share their post or comment, make sure that it's because what they say is of value to you. Spread it out over the next 30 days and don't be tempted to overdo it. The last thing you want is being known as a "stalker". What you're doing here is being noticed by them, so when you send them your idea, you're not a stranger anymore.

Step #3: Connection

Once you've warmed them up on social media, the next step is to send them an email. When you write the email, remember in Chapter 1 I shared that the key is to make it all about them.

So in your email, while proposing the collaboration, create an irresistible value that they can get by collaborating with you. Remember to compliment them genuinely and create that warmth. You can say something like:

You're doing amazing things!

I'd love to collaborate with you on this project/idea ____________. (what's your idea about)

Here's what you're going to get from our collaboration: ________________. (list the benefits/value/results that they are going to get)

A little about me: _____________. (3-5 lines about you—make sure you brag about your authority)

*Would that be something that you're interes*ted *in?*

(Your Name)

Remember, make the idea about all the exciting things that they're going to get out of this collaboration and you're likely to win them over, or at the very least a response with "tell me more".

Offer something that is a win-win for both of you. Highlight profits for them, but also be clear on what it is that you want to get from them. Let's say for every referral that comes from that project, you can give them a referral of X amount of money, or you can offer them with a high value service. Be creative!

Remember to have an agreement ready when they say YES! Always seal it with a black and white—with both of your signatures on it so that everything is clear. Once you have that deal, remember that you also have to nurture that relationship because people buy people.

People work with people they can trust. If you say something on merit, so when you promise to do something, make sure that you deliver it. This will solidify your credibility and trust factor with them. Talk is cheap, but action is the deal break. Be authentic and real and honor your word. Trust is one of the most important keys in any relationship.

Conclusion

So think about who the tribe leader is, not just anybody, but the ones that have the ideal target audience that is a perfect fit for you and your brand and vice versa. Then send them a pitch, propose a win-win collaboration, but at the same time, make it all about them. And then deliver what you promised.

Power Summary

Fill in the blanks and answer the questions.

1. Find a tribe leader who has __________________.
2. What is step #1 when approaching a tribe leader?
3. Make it all about _________.

Key Actions

Here are the key actions that can help you move forward.

1. Search for an influencer that you're interested to collaborate with.
2. Check out their social media or website.

3. Write down three things that you feel you can offer them that will be a WIN-WIN for you both, for example, a masterclass, book project, interview on your podcast, training, etc.

To access the action plan and materials for this chapter, go to:

https://www.izdiharjamil.com/resources

The Power of Association

"The quickest way to build trust with a new audience is through the power of association."

— Dr. Izdihar Jamil

Growth

"Being uncomfortable is part of growth. It means you're living!"

— Dr. Izdihar Jamil

Growth is part of the process of having a business and life in general. You have to be prepared for growth. More importantly, be open to it and be ready to move toward it with minimal resistance.

Otherwise, you're not just going to be stuck and stressed out, but you can become a slave to the monster that you created. Because you simply don't have the capacity and bandwidth to grow or take care of the requests that come in.

There are a few factors in your business that you need to put the foundation on to help your business grow and expand with ease. The first step that can help you is by learning new skills.

New Skills

As your business grows, it shows you the demands of your clients—what they're wanting, and the results that they're looking to achieve. Look for clues that will tell you whether you need to make things simpler, faster, let things go, or add new things. It is very likely that your clients' demands will change over time, and if you choose to be stagnant, your business may not survive it.

For example, when *Netflix* was first introduced, the people at Blockbuster said there's no way people are going to want *Netflix*. They want the experience of coming to the store and choosing the latest movie to watch. Blockbuster didn't change.

A few years on, *Netflix* has revolutionized the way people watch movies by streaming it right to their living rooms on demand. As for Blockbuster, they didn't survive the shift and are no longer in business.

Now if you want to keep moving forward and keep reaching new heights, you have to grow yourself consistently and learn new skills rapidly so that you can accommodate all the demands of your clients. Listen to the clues that your clients are giving you and then expand yourself and your business to accommodate it.

Think of it as your commitment to taking your clients on a journey that can best help them in realizing their dreams and goals. What you want is for them to buy from you over and over again. That's how you create sustainability in your business. In order for you to do so, you need to acquire new skills as you expand your business.

For example, my clients wanted to be the go-to authority in their niche. One of the ways to do it is by writing a book and becoming a Bestselling Author. Writing and publishing a bestseller book is not part of my initial skill set.

But I met an investment in learning everything that I could from the best expert in the business so I can provide this service for my clients. I learned about editing, publishing, graphics, marketing, and running a bestseller campaign.

I created a team with the best expert in each field to help me give the best experience to my clients. Today, I have helped over 100 people to become a bestselling author with my publishing system.

The biggest feedback that I've received from my clients is that *"You made it so easy!"* All my clients have to focus on is writing the best book that they can, and my team and I will take care of the rest.

There are many ways that you can get new skills:

- Hire a coach.
- Attend a seminar or training.
- Learn from a course.
- Read a book.
- Shadowing an expert.

For me, the best way that I learn is when I work 1:1 with the top expert in the industry. After that, I just keep on practicing until I have gained mastery in the area.

Having a Team

Another part of sustaining growth is having a team that can support your expansion. As you're starting up, you may not need a team due to minimal funds available as well as the common "one-man-show" idealism.

However, there will be a point when you'll experience an overwhelming demand for your service as you become really good at what you do. There are so many hours in a day and the last thing you want is to burn out and become a slave to your own business. You want to have the growth, the freedom, and have highly skilled people who can do the work for you.

In some of the things, you may need to invest some time in training, because they require specialized skills, like high ticket sales and lead generation. While other things like admin work and data entry may require minimal work as these are relatively easy tasks.

One of the best things that I've done as my business grows is hiring a virtual assistant and a social media manager. My virtual assistant helps in taking care of any admin and repetitive work. My social media manager helps to nurture my leads and lead them to my client conversion system. It frees up my time so I can focus on the most important things for my business.

The other thing that helped with my business growth is hiring a bookkeeper or accountant for my business. This way I know that all the bookkeeping stuff is being taken care of by a professional and it is done correctly. I don't have to stress myself out in learning the different elements of the accounting software.

Of course, at the end of the day, you are still responsible for your own numbers. Make sure that you check their work every time to make sure things are done correctly. To do this, you would need to acquire the skills of reading your own financial statements. Once you have this, you can see how your numbers flow or don't flow. You can also easily spot any abnormality in your accounting.

If you feel that at any point a particular team member isn't performing as well as you're expecting them to, don't just make assumptions. Have a conversation with them and work with them so that they've got clarity on what to do. If, for some reason, their performance is still poor, you may choose to let them go and find another person who may be a good fit.

Allow for yourself and your business to be supported by the best people so you can have the energy to be the best at what you do.

You can check out Fiverr or Upwork to look for highly skilled people to help with your business.

Set an Intention

How do you get the best people in your business? I usually start off by setting an intention.

For example, after the baby munchkin was born, I knew that I couldn't go on back-to-back sales calls anymore. Baby munchkin is my priority. Yes, I could take him with me during my calls, but it also means that I have to split my concentration between my clients and baby munchkin and that's exhausting. It means that I have to work double or triple efforts just to concentrate.

So I knew that I needed to have team members to help me with taking care of the sales calls. I set the intention of having the best person to help me. I prayed and asked God to guide me and to show me the right person.

Soon, the right person shows up, and I am now blessed to have amazing people to help do the sales calls for me. They are people who believe in my products and are literally right in front of me. They are the walking and talking advertisements for my services.

So set your intention so that the best person who aligns with your principles and values is shown to you. And when they do, hold on to them because they are going to help explode your business!

Automation

I love automation! It can help to run your business without you having to be there. You can optimize all of your businesses or some parts of your business by using automation as a tool.

I would recommend that you start with a section of your business.

The thing with automation is that you have to test it out over and over again to see if it's giving you the result that you want. For example, let's say you have a Masterclass that you do manually, or a course that you teach manually. Once you've run it to the point of conversion, only then would you set up an automation process to it. You can use software like

WebinarJam to set things up so that it can run with or without you being there. That's really cool.

So have a look at your business and what process in your business that you can automate. For example, your email sequence, webinar, masterclass, or opt in. Simplify it to the point that it's converting or producing the results that you want. Then look for a software, a system, or a person who can help you to leverage it for you. That's how you set up automation.

Let's say you have a set of emails. Once people register with you, they'll receive an email sequence that will lead them to a conversion to one of your services. The key here is making sure that those sets of email sequences are converting.

Once you know what the email sequences are, set them up on automation. I use ActiveCampaign software to schedule the email sequences. That means that you don't have to manually send an email and the best part, the email sequence is being taken care of by the software.

For example, when people sign up for my "Top Authority Activation Retreat" on my website at www.izdiharjamil.com and enter their details, I have already connected the data entry with my mailing list on ActiveCampaign. So now when I want to send them an email, I can do so with just one click.

To take it to the next level, once people register, it'll activate a list of email sequences designed to convert them to one of my products and services. This means that I only have to do it once and I don't have to even be there for it to happen. Remember, you need to test it out to make sure that those email sequences or the process is converting. Otherwise, it'll be a waste of your time and resources. Consequently, rather than nurturing your leads, it can create a negative experience for them.

Technology

Now let's talk about using technology. I know some of you may be a little scared to use technology and that's totally normal. The extra learning curve and the familiarization of technology can often be stressful.

Even though I have a Ph.D. in Computer Science and, as you can guess, I'm technologically savvy. Learning a new technology isn't something that I'm excited about. However, in certain cases, the benefits of technology outweigh the costs associated with implementing it, so it's really worth it.

Here is a list of the top software and technologies that I use in my business. Some of them are free, some are paid for. It's a good starting point for you to check it out:

- ***Canva*** (https://canva.com). *Canva* is a great tool to help you out with your graphics related tasks, like graphics to make posters, your *Facebook* page, and your book cover idea, etc.

- ***WebinarJam*** (https://home.webinarjam.com). A great tool to run my training and Masterclass on demand. I just need to record it once and let it play. The software will take care of the whole onboarding and running the Masterclass without me.

- ***Teachable*** (https://teachable.com). It's where I used to host my online course, and there's even a free version of it too.

- ***Stripe*** (https://stripe.com). A fantastic tool that helps me take payments online or on my website or even issue an invoice.

- ***ActiveCampaign*** (https://www.activecampaign.com/). Email marketing, automation, and CRM tools to create customer experience. It has many integrations apps with websites, *Google* sheets, and can help simplify your process.

- **Livestream** (https://livestream.com/). Helps to run pre-recorded videos LIVE on my social media.

- **PostPlanner** (https://www.postplanner.com/). I can literally post across various social media platforms, such as *Facebook, Instagram, LinkedIn,* and *Twitter*, with just one post! It saves me so much time having to log in to various social media accounts.

- **Quickbooks** (https://quickbooks.intuit.com/). I use *Quickbooks* to keep my accounting up to date. I can see how my company is doing by the minute. The best part is that my accountant can access it directly and knows what needs to be done with my business.

I hope that you'll at least try one or two new technologies that can help you to grow your business. Yes, it can be scary, but just take one small step at a time. Remember, the benefits of using technology versus doing it manually outweigh the challenges of not having it.

Power Summary

Let's review the key points in this chapter.

1. Fill in the blanks. Growth is ________________.
2. Name one way that you can learn new skills.
3. Name one software that I used in my business.

Key Actions

Here are your steps to help you move forward in your business.

1. Name one area in your business that you can automate.
2. Outsource one repetitive task to a software or a team member.
3. Research one software that can be helpful in your business.

To access the action plan and materials for this chapter, go to:

https://www.izdiharjamil.com/resources

Growth

"Being uncomfortable is part of growth. It means you're living!"

— Dr. Izdihar Jamil

Loving Sales

"I love sales with a passion! It's my opportunity to help others."

— Dr. Izdihar Jamil

I used to hate sales with a passion.

I remembered when I was in a leadership program, I was supposed to make a phone call to a potential client. Before I even dialed the number, I said...*Please don't be there. Please don't be there. Please don't be there.*

My heart started to beat so fast. I couldn't breathe. My chest tightened. I just didn't want to do it. Yes, it was that scary for me. I used to feel like I was holding my breath the entire phone call. And when it would end, that's the moment that I could finally breathe.

What's worse was that I would actually feel guilty during sales calls because I believed that in my mind, I was taking people's money and ripping them off. There were moments when I felt so guilty that I just gave things away for free at the cost of me losing money in my business.

The reality is that if you want to have a successful and profitable business, your business needs to generate an income. How? By making a lot of sales in exchange for a value, products, or services that can help solve people's problems.

The number one reason why businesses fail is because they aren't making the sales or the money required to create a healthy and sustainable business. Whether you hate sales or love them, sales is the key in your business.

Even if you have an amazing product, if you're not making money from it, your business isn't going to survive. Sales is key. Money in the bank is key. Cash flow in your business is key.

It's time to shift your mindset from hating sales to loving sales with a passion. Think of sales as just an opportunity or a conversation for you to help other people to live their best lives from your expertise.

Often, the reason why people hate sales is because they associate sales with their self-worth or disempowering belief systems. For example, by doing sales, I'm forcing people to buy from me. Or I'm just bad at sales and when I don't make sales, it means that I'm a failure.

The first step is to let go of those disempowering belief systems. You're doing a disservice to yourself by hanging on to it. The second step is to see sales as a "neutral" part of a process in your business. The third step is learning to fall in love with sales.

Just imagine the lives of the people that you can help just by offering your products and services. The access to that is a successful sales conversion.

Purpose of Sales

I used to think that sales were a bad thing because I felt like I was ripping people off. I was somehow pressuring them by being sales-y and pushy.

But when I understood what the purpose of sales is, it completely changed me. If you take a look at your everyday life, you are naturally doing sales in your life. For example, if you want your husband to help you take out the trash, you're engaging in a sales process with him to convert him into doing the task.

When you want your kids to eat the fruit and vegetables or brush their teeth, that's another form of sales. Now, of course, you're not exchanging money for these tasks. You're exchanging them with something else and enrolling them to something that can create a win-win for both of you.

So if you think about it, you are naturally doing sales every day of your life. And that shouldn't be hard for you to transfer back to your business. It should be easy, because it's something you've been doing since you were a baby. What does a baby do when they want milk? It cries, and that's the way babies are making sales and getting the attention of the parents to give them food.

You are a natural sales superstar. You were born with it. And the thing is, when it comes to sales in business, this seems to be a block. *How did it happen? Why did it happen?*

So I want you to have an understanding and shift your mindset on the purpose of sales. Some people hate sales passionately, despite having a business.

Before, I couldn't say the word 'sales' without getting anxious. Now, I can say it multiple times without getting triggered. I've trained myself to fall in love with sales. I love it with a passion because I see it as an opportunity for me to help others in living their dreams in exchange for my expertise.

I see sales as just a conversation that has two things—enrollment and registration. You're enrolling people to a particular vision, to a clear result, to the transformation that they desire. Registration comes when they sign the form—the signing, filling the names on the dotted line—and then they give you the money. That's when the registration happens.

I want you to think about the mindset of sales. Be open to this new way of thinking. Sales is just an opportunity or a tool to help people solve their problems. It is neither good nor bad, right or wrong. It has nothing to do with ripping them off or pushing them to do something that they don't want to do. Trust that people can make up their own decision on what's best for them and that you're just the right person to help them manifest their dreams.

For example, when one of my good friends wasn't feeling very well, I cooked food for her and I delivered it to her, because I wanted to help and make things easy for her and her family. I know she was having difficulty cooking for her family during her sickness. I was helping her solve her problem by cooking and delivering the food to her. She got to rest, and I got to take care of her.

It's the same with sales. All that you're doing is helping to make things easy for them, and you help them to solve their problems.

So if you come from that space, how can you not be a sales superstar? How can you not have pride, joy, and commitment in what you do? Because you are helping people solve their problems and make life easy for them. You're like the answer to their prayers.

It's All About Them

One of the biggest misconceptions about sales is thinking that your ideas and solutions are what your customers need. In other words, you're saying *"This is what I think they need."* when in reality, they may not need that because you haven't even asked them what they want.

When you're doing the sales, you have to remember that it's all about them—that's the number one rule in sales. It isn't about you. The key focus is them: your clients and their desires.

What people are buying into is the transformation and results that you can help them to achieve. You're selling them the best possible future, taking them from point A to point B. That's what people buy into—the brightness of the future.

And how can they have that?

By engaging in your products, services, and expertise.

For example, a client of mine wanted to build her authority fast by having endorsements from the media. So I created a media publicity for her that had her being featured on FOX, NBC, CBS, and hundreds of other media outlets showcasing her as the go-to expert in her field. Having globally trusted organizations endorsing her business instantly elevated her status as the authority in her field, making it easy for her potential clients to say YES to her.

So she gets the transformation from a self-proclaimed expert to being the go-to expert in her field backed up by hundreds of other globally trusted organizations. In exchange for the service, I charged her a fee for my expertise in getting her that result.

Meeting of the Heart

Sales is just an honest conversation that is the meeting of the hearts. It's that simple. It's not about ripping off people; it's not about pushing them. It's just about an honest conversation that is a meeting of the hearts.

So in a conversation, I love to explore and paint the picture with my clients by asking questions such as:

What are your dreams?

When you have that, what would be possible in your business and life?

When someone says that you changed their life, how do you feel?

And then you can share with them details about what you do. When both your hearts and logic are in alignment, that's where the YES comes from. There's an exchange of money for your services.

Now remember, you don't want everybody to be your client.

What you want are people who are in alignment with your vision and in line with the energy. People who are committed; people who are hungry for success; people who are emotionally, financially, physically, and mentally ready to work with you. And in return, you can give them that 100 percent commitment to help them solve the problems.

Now, isn't that more exciting than thinking of sales as being pushy or sales-y?

It's just a meeting of the hearts. It's not so different from you inviting people to come over to your party or going to a restaurant that you really love. It is similar in the sense that you're attracting the right people to come and buy your products and services.

And that's how you get people excited about things, and they can see that, *Oh my God, she can help solve my problem. She can help me to do this and that. I'm going to be moving from point A to point B. And she really cares about me.*

That's how I was able to shift things: by holding onto my new definition of sales—a meeting of the hearts—so I can help make their dreams come alive. It's now fun when I go to a sales call; it's like me having a chat with one of my best friends.

Regardless of what happens, I know that I've done my best.

Authority

Another factor that can play into the decision making is credibility. Do you have the credibility to give them the results that they want? For example, doctors have the "MD" title behind their names that gives them the right authority to help people in the healthcare industry.

Authority and credibility create the know-like-love-trust factor that is important during conversion. Your clients want to know that you're the best person who can help them. By having certain types of credibility, you can give them that peace of mind that you can deliver.

For example, one of my credentials that put me as the #1 go-to expert in my field is that I have been featured on *Forbes* and *TED* platforms. Both are prestigious and iconic brands—only the best of the best are featured there. So when people come to me, they know that I've got the right credentials to back me up. That creates trust even before we have a conversion because my brand has a solid reputation.

Think of it this way, which one would your clients rather choose, a self-proclaimed expert or someone who has been featured on *Forbes* and the *TED* platform?

Exactly! The one who has been featured on *Forbes* and *TED* because those iconic brands carry a lot of weight in solidifying your position as the expert.

So start thinking about how you can have those credentials in your business too to make it easy for your clients to say YES to you.

The Rejection

In my book *Yes I Can!*, I shared about the power projection. I talked about how I was rejected for six years for my Ph.D. work, specifically in having one of my articles published at the biggest conference in my field. But because of my persistence in holding on to my dream, one day, I received the news that my publication was accepted and then I was presenting my work on a stage at a prestigious conference.

Rejection is a part of the success process of guiding us toward our destination.

Now, the thing is, we make it a big deal when people say no to us because it can bring up a lot of old wounds and things that happened to us in the past when we were rejected. We don't feel good enough. We don't feel loved. We don't feel worthy. It brings up those emotions and wounds. Suddenly, rejection brings the feeling of shame and failure in our lives.

So I want you to know that a no is just a *no*. It doesn't mean anything but a no. You can get a lot of pain and suffering when you attach stories to it, which is not healthy for you or your business.

So if you think about it, you're going to be getting either a yes or no. Nobody is going to get all yes, yes, yes. That's just not practical. I've never heard anybody who says yes all the time. People can say no. And that's OK.

That's part of the process. Just know that rejection is a blessing because it's just a correction toward your destined process.

Be a Leader

When you're having a sales conversation, you have to create yourself as the alpha or the leader during the conversion. There's a saying in sales that you have to "lead the lead". Because once you lose that leadership role and become a follower, it'll be challenging to close the deal.

One of the ways to create a warm leadership is by stating right in the beginning how the call is going to go. For example, you can say, *"How the call is going to go is that I'll be sharing with you what I'm best known for. Then I'll be asking you some questions, and we'll be exploring your vision together. Once I know your dreams, I'll be offering you some ideas on how you can get results. If I feel that we're a good fit, I'll be sharing with you my ideas on how we can take it to the next step. How does that sound to you?"*

Now, we've set a foundation on how the call will go and that you'll be leading them through the conversion. So there are no surprises.

Once you get them to a point where they are interested and ready to move forward, create a space where you can have that conversation with integrity. Don't just jump into it without preparing them. If you do, you can feel that they'll put up a wall and it'll be harder for your message to reach their hearts.

You can say something like, *"Based on what you said, I've got an idea that can help you hit your dreams. Would you be open to hear me out?"*

Once they have given you their permission, you can go ahead and share your ideas, products, or services. This way, their walls are down and they are open to receiving your help.

Irresistible Offer

What you need to hook them in and make the offer look super attractive in the sales process is to add something really, really irresistible. It has to be something that's so hard to resist and a no-brainer for them to say YES to, because they fear missing out on that irresistible offer.

For example, a client of mine who'll be having her book out wants to be on TV as part of her publicity campaign. I know that she's a busy mom and entrepreneur. So instead of teaching her how to get that TV opportunity, I offered a done-for-you service in which I'll do the work to get her that TV feature.

I also know that she wants the message of her book to be seen in multiple places. As part of the irresistible offer, I add several booked-for-you podcast interviews—she just has to show up and share her stories.

I also offered full feature on highly influential magazines and publications, both in digital and print versions. Some of the publications that I offered have 1 million views—now that's a WOW factor, right? That way, she can maximize the publicity of her book and business across multiple platforms.

So in your business, think about how you can package your offer and add things on to make it irresistible.

Pre-Sell

I've mentioned it before in my previous chapter that one of the keys to successful sales is that before you develop the whole product, test it out first to see if the market wants it. One of the ways to do that is for you to pre-sell things or pre-selling your idea.

Though make sure you do it with integrity in the sense that when they say yes, you can deliver the results for them. And for the sake of clarity, at least brainstorm that idea first before you test it out.

You don't have to know all the hundred steps or the hundred details of it, but you need at least a foundation before you pre-sell it. For example, you know what your idea is about, how it can help them, and what are the things involved. So when a person says yes and you take their money, you make sure that you can deliver that with integrity.

For example, I created a 12-month program on how female leaders can share their voice on prestigious platforms and create a huge impact on their business and society. It's also a system on solidifying their position as the #1 go-to expert in their fields. I call it my Diamond program.

In that program, I included items that I have personally found to be effective in rapidly building authority. I help them by elevating their brand through conscious PR. For example, I've included a bestselling book project, TV, *Forbes*, magazines, and *TED*.

I have my own expertise in helping people get those results and, for areas that I'm lacking, I have the best team that can help deliver those results. So that's how I can offer it with integrity and when people say YES, I'm ready to go because all the team members and systems are in place.

One of the ways that you can pre-sell a product is that you test it out in the market. You can put a social media post about it or you can reach out to a few people that you've personally handpicked that you feel are a good fit with the product and services. Then you have a conversation with them and see what they say, what their feedback is, if it's a yes or a no.

From there, you simply tweak your ideas and offers until it's a perfect fit for you and them.

I'll give you an example of a book project. Usually when I come up with a book idea, for example, with my book *Women Who Lead*, I create a mock cover for it, just a simple visual so people can see my vision.

Then I put a post on my social media and put two covers with different backgrounds with the caption, "*Which cover do you love the best? Black or Pink?*"

What that creates is a conversation and a great way to attract the lead that may be interested in the book project.

And what I saw was that there was a lot of engagement. People were coming back to say, *Oh, I love your title; I love your idea. I can't wait to know more about it. Tell me more.*

With that, I knew that it's going to be converting because you can sell what the market wants. We pre-sell ideas. Know what your idea is. You can gain clarity by brainstorming what it can look like, what it's going to deliver, and how it's going to help people. Then reach out to people on social media or hand-pick a few people to have the conversation about it. And then you go from there.

One more way that you can pre-sell is something that I call the Love formula. The Love formula is awesome and is highly converting. The Love formula is a fantastic way to test things, to see if people are engaging with it.

All you do is say, *"Would you love to ____________ (result)?"*

So ask questions like,

Would you love to be a bestselling author in 30 days?

Would you love to be featured on Forbes?

Would you love to be featured on TED?

Would you love to be featured on TV and in the media?

Would you love to get five new clients this month?

Would you love to be making 10K this month?

Would you love to lose 30 pounds in 30 days?

Those that are engaging in your post, invite them for a chat to explore the idea further with them. If you feel that both of you are a good fit, offer them an opportunity to work with you in exchange for an investment as you deliver the results.

Practice

You have to practice being in multiple sales conversations because sales is a learnable skill.

It's like any other skill, such as cooking. You don't suddenly just cook. You need to practice the chopping, the sauteing, the frying, the measurements, etc. You have to practice that muscle to make it efficient. Even though you are naturally born with the skills of sales, you still need to practice it over and over again to be confident in your skills.

Michael Phelps, who is one of the most commendable Olympic athletes, is a swimmer. He has won many gold medals at the Olympics. Michael Phelps practices six days a week, six to eight hours a day. For years, he's been swimming and been committed to the practice of being the best swimmer. He's been swimming since he was five or six years old, but he still practices so that he is the best at what he does. That's how he's been labeled as one of the greatest Olympians, having won so many gold medals.

It's the same with you. You're like an Olympian, even though you're not getting paid like the Olympians. And what do Olympic athletes do? They practice all the time. You just need to practice the skill over and over again. So even if you mess up, that's okay. Reflect back on what works, what doesn't work, and then learn from that. Every master was once a disaster, so just chill and keep going.

Sales Structure

Personally, I don't use a sales script anymore. I now use a really simple sales structure that was taught to me by two of the best sales coaches that I have met—Vanessa Moss and Carly Hope.

I would start off either by creating a connection or complimenting them. This is important before jumping to the sales conversation because in the first instance, people are really nervous and you can be nervous, too. So when you mention something common to compliment them and try to relate, it just settles the energy a bit.

Then I would go on and get clarity on the intention of the call. I usually say something like, "*We could just chat the whole day. But let's come back to the intention of the call. Tell me, what is your intention for the call? Or what is your expectation from the call?*"

This way, they can communicate comfortably about what they want.

They are giving you clues about their dreams and desires. Then you can prepare yourself for how you can best structure your call.

Once I've got clarity on the intention, I would then lay out the structure on how the call is going to go. I say something like, *"Awesome! So this is how the call is going to go. I'm going to be asking you some questions so that I can understand your vision better. I will then ask you questions about where you are now and what your biggest dreams are. Then I'm going to offer you some tips that can help you. If I feel that we're a good fit, I'll offer you some ideas on how we can take the next step. Sounds cool?"*

After this statement, they usually say, *"Yeah, that's cool."*

When you work like this, you're setting down the foundation of how the call is going to go. You've settled their nerves and have been given the "green light" to move forward. Remember, you have to be the leader. You're going to lead the call. This is how it works. You tell them they can sit back, and you take charge. Once you've done that, you go on asking them questions about their goal.

When you feel that they're ready for the next step, use the Love formula to create an opening to your offer. For example, *"You've told me that you wanted X, Y and Z. So tell me, would you love to be a* TEDx *speaker?"*

And they're either going to say yes or no. Most likely they are going to say YES to that since that is their dream that they've told you that they wanted to achieve.

When they say yes, you can say something like, "*That's fantastic*! *Would you be open for me to share with you some ideas on how you can do that?"*

At this point, remember to wait for them to say yes, so you'll have their permission to explore things further. So that means they can relax and are open to receiving your offer. You're not pushing or pressuring anybody. You have asked for their permission to share the details of your offer.

Power Summary

Let's review the key points in this chapter.

1. Rejection is a _______________.
2. What's the biggest thing that any business needs to survive?
3. What's the #1 rule of sales?

Key Actions

Here are your steps to help you move forward in your business.

1. Craft a converting Love formula. Would you love to ________ (results)?
2. What's one idea that you can pre-sell right now?
3. What's one offer that you have that you can add an irresistible element to?

To access the action plan and materials for this chapter, go to:

https://www.izdiharjamil.com/resources

The Non-Negotiable

"Doing your non-negotiable consistently is what builds a solid foundation for your business."

— Dr. Izdihar Jamil

Part of building a successful business is to have something that I call a non-negotiable. A non-negotiable is something that you have to do every day, or at least on a consistent basis that serves as the foundation in your business.

Brian Tracy, who is a top leader in human potential development, says that *"One of the keys to success is to work every day."*

And I was like, *"I don't want to work every day. I want to have a weekend off with my family."*

And Brian firmly says, *"Every day."*

And so I did follow through with my non-negotiable every day. There's something about doing a particular routine every day that just creates an ongoing momentum in your business. You don't have to do 20-30 things every day. That's just going to stress you out and set you up for failure.

In the book *The Richest Man In Babylon*, the key to being rich and wealthy is to do simple things but doing so consistently. That is what I meant by non-negotiable, simple things that you do everyday that set the foundation of your business. A thriving business is built upon a solid foundation, and it starts with your non-negotiable.

For me, I practice three types of non-negotiables in my life and business—yourself, business, and family.

Yourself

Taking care of you is the most important thing because without you, there'll be no family or community, and there certainly won't be any business.

Here are some of my non-negotiables on a daily basis:

- Starting my day with a prayer and reading the Holy Quran.
- Drinking 8 glasses of water.
- Taking my supplements.
- Having breakfast.
- Walking in my garden barefoot and doing grounding work.
- Do something that I enjoy, like reading a book.

We can sometimes get so occupied by working on things that we forget to work on ourselves. Always have some time and do something special, especially for you. It can be anything from a five-minute walk that you take once a day, a special place you go to, or once a week, you treat yourself to a meal out. Just take care of yourself, whether it's about giving you a facial or a massage.

You treat self-care as a non-negotiable to honor yourself. The key here is finding what works best for you and stick with it on a daily basis if possible.

Business

In your business, what is the non-negotiable that you want to set up that can help to create a thriving business? For example, my non-negotiables in my business are:

- I post on social media every day.
- I attract clients every day.
- I make a sale every day.

Don't worry if some of the non-negotiables that you've set up don't materialize or aren't being fulfilled. For example, one of your non-negotiable is to make sales every day and you don't make a sale today. All you have to do is let go of any attachments or stories like *"I'm a failure"* or

"I'm bad at what I do". Then recommit the next day. All you're doing is practicing that muscle every day and soon something that is hard or feels unachievable will be like a new normal for you.

You'll be moving closer and closer toward your non-negotiable to the point that at one divine moment, you and your non-negotiables will meet and become a daily reality.

Clients

Having the best clients is the key to a joyful and thriving business. You can't work with anybody, because a client that is not in alignment with your principles and values can become an expensive investment to your time, health, energy, and mental wellness.

So figure out what's a non-negotiable that you're looking for in your clients. For example, one of the non-negotiable would be to work with clients who have a positive mindset or people who would honor their commitment. If they say they're going to do something, they'll deliver. It can also be about people who will respect and honor you, who have a kind heart.

I have a policy that if people were to miss a session with me, then they book a call with me. I would tell them straight that I understand. You have to give people the benefit of the doubt, right?

> *You missed this appointment. I hope you're OK. But just to let you know, you have one more opportunity with me. If you miss the call without prior communication then you will have no more opportunity with me for this year.*

You're setting a clear boundary on your business procedures. I used to have this scarcity mindset that I'll lose people if I'm setting these boundaries. Then I've discovered that the people who are serious about their success and in working with me will show up. People will also tend to respect you more because you have a backbone in sticking to your principles. There are abundant clients who will love working with you, who are the perfect fit, so just be open and ready to welcome them.

Think about it this way. You're the prize. You're the prize in the business. You're offering something so valuable and something so priceless that people are hungry for it. Those who value you and themselves will show up. It is how nature works.

Working Hours

Setting up reasonable working hours for yourself and your business creates a foundation for a strong physical and mental health. The last thing you want is being burned out because you're working all the time with little rest or time-off.

For example, your working hours can be from 9 to 5, Monday to Friday. And you don't work on weekends, no matter if your clients call you, email you, or text you. You do not respond out of your working hours.

Should your clients become persistent, you can say something like this and then let it go.

Thank you for reaching out, but just know that I do not respond outside the working hours. I'll look into it as soon as I'm back in the office.

Family

My family is a big part of my life. My husband and my three children are the biggest reason why I do what I do. However, if you're not being mindful, you can work yourself into exhaustion by taking care of your family.

A psychologist once told me when I interviewed her on my podcast *Yes I Can!* that if you always put your children first, you can potentially create a "narcissistic" behavior. In other words, your children would have the mindset of thinking "me first" and may not have the awareness of other people's well-being.

So figure out a balance where there are times when you come first and then there are times when your family comes first.

Some of my non-negotiables for my family include:

- My children would clear up the dishwasher every day.
- My husband would help me do the dishes every day.
- On Saturday, my husband would prepare breakfast.
- On Sunday, my kids would make their own breakfast.
- On Sunday, my husband would make lunch and dinner.

What are some simple non-negotiables that you can create with your family?

Power Summary

Let's review the key points in this chapter.

1. What do I mean by non-negotiables?
2. List one non-negotiable that I have for myself that you can relate to.
3. List one non-negotiable that I have for my business that you can relate to.

Key Actions

Here are your actions steps to help you move forward in your business.

1. List one non-negotiable for yourself.
2. List one non-negotiable for your business.
3. List one non-negotiable for your family.

To access the action plan and materials for this chapter, go to:

https://www.izdiharjamil.com/resources

The Non-Negotiables

"Doing your non-negotiables consistently is what builds a solid foundation for your business."

— Dr. Izdihar Jamil

Tweaking

"Perfection is an illusion. It's a trap. Let it go!"

— Dr. Izdihar Jamil

It doesn't have to be perfect. It just has got to be done. Just start, even if you feel like you're not ready, tell yourself that you are, and just begin the work. Perfection is an illusion. It's a trap that is going to hold you down.

The longer you hold on to it, the stronger it becomes and then suddenly years would pass, and you would still be in the same position, trying to create the "perfect" thing.

Let Go of Perfection

When I was working on my Ph.D., I had to write a paper for a top publication that is the epitome of my Ph.D. work. So this is like, huge. It is a form of validating my four years of research.

So I worked really hard on it and when my Ph.D. professor asked me, "*Is it ready yet?*" I said, "*I'm still working on it.*"

This happened several times because I wanted my work to be so perfect that when he takes one look at it, he'll be blown away.

When I was finally ready with it, I sent it over, thinking that it'll be flawless.

But guess what?

He sent it back with more corrections. And that's when I learned that perfection is just an illusion. Even the best writer or researcher would take several iterations before finalizing their work. Creating something to be the best it can be is just a process that requires changes and revisions.

You're always tweaking, adjusting them, modifying, changing them, and deleting various parts of the work. And then you would do it again and again until there comes a point where you feel that things just click. And that's when you let go and trust that everything is going to be OK. That your hard work will pay off.

Success isn't about just doing things one time, and that's it. Success comes in the listening, tweaking, the changing, the modifying, and the adjustment of things over and over again. It isn't about winning. It's about the number of times that you're willing to get up and do the hard work.

That's the principle that I want you to master in your business. The art of tweaking things over and over again. Rather than focusing on perfection, just focusing on making things better and better.

For example, Apple has released so many versions of the iPhone that I lost count. Apple doesn't wait until it has the perfect iPhone before releasing it. It releases one version after the other, and each one is an improvement of the previous model.

It's the same in your business, whether it's your website, your sales page, your social media posting, or your offer. Just start with whatever you have. Then focus on making it better and better.

In my business, as part of my lead generation strategy, I would post on social media every day. One of the post I did was *"Who in my FB is an awesome coach? Say ME!"* I noticed that I got very little engagement, despite my *Facebook* profile being full of coaches.

Then someone dropped a comment saying, *"I think I'm an awesome coach"*. So that gives me a clue that even though there are a lot of coaches in my social media, they may not think that they are awesome or they may think that they may not be there yet.

So I tweaked the post and removed the word "awesome" from my message. So it's now *"Who in my FB is a coach? Say ME!"* By tweaking that one single word based on the feedback, it quickly increased my engagement because people now didn't feel threatened by the word *awesome*. So I learned to keep things neutral or not putting a label when I'm calling out for a particular group of people in my network.

Just Do It

Often when we have to do something, especially when we have to put ourselves in a vulnerable position, be aware of the self-sabotaging behavior that might occur. It can be in the form of distracting yourself to do other things, it can be in talking yourself out of it, or it can be in the form of creating something else that takes priority over it.

So when you're actually feeling something like, *"God, I'm not good at this" or "I need to change this first to look like this before I can share it" or "I might as well give up because it's just so bad".*

I'm here to tell you that it doesn't matter how bad, ugly, and unfinished it may look. Just start, even if you don't feel like you're ready. Just go and get it done because there is a sense of power when you complete things. Every master was once a disaster so don't worry, darlings, you're on the right track! And the best part is that the more you practice, the better you'll become. As time goes, it'll take you much faster to complete things than when you first started.

I remember that in my first book project, I was invited to participate in *She Made It Happen*. Until then, I had never contributed to a book project before. Yes, I have written a thesis and other publications for my Ph.D. but they are so different—the style, theme, and the audience.

And I was like, *"Oh, I'm not sure that I can even write a good chapter. I don't think I have anything valuable to share."*

At that moment, I had just moved to America and was in the beginning stage of my online entrepreneurship journey. I had the desire to make money while taking care of my two young kids. I only had a couple of clients, and I didn't think that my journey was worthy of being shared in a book with other successful women.

Even though I didn't feel that I was fully ready at that time, I just said YES. All I did was just shared the truth about my journey—my challenges, lessons, and success up to the point where I am. I just took my reader on a journey, showing them how I got from point A to point B. I didn't overthink it. I didn't have to hide because that is the truth about my journey.

And the response has been overwhelming. Not only it gave me the confidence of my skill set, but it also anchored my beliefs that I was meant to help other women share their voice without prejudice. Now, I have 10 books that are #1 in multiple countries. I have also helped over 100 people become bestselling authors in the last two years alone. That wouldn't have happened if I had waited for "perfection" or "when I'm ready".

Just start, even before you feel ready, and keep moving forward one step at a time.

I'm not saying that I'm better than anyone else, but I'm saying by letting go of my perfection, I am able to move forward despite it being messy. I'm prepared to take the next steps, and it doesn't matter where I am. The way I am now is whole, perfect, and complete, the way I am and the way I am not.

For example, in your business, just write something and post it on social media. The more you do it, the more you learn. If you do it every day, you can only get better and better. And the time it takes you is going to get shorter and shorter. The same thing with any part of your business. Just focus on being better and effective as you practice.

Power Summary

Let's review the key points in this chapter.

1. Fill in the blank. Perfection is an _______________.
2. Just focus on getting better.
3. Be prepared to tweak things over and over again. Success is messy, and that's OK.

Key Actions

Here are your steps to help you move forward in your business.

1. What's one thing that you can do today that you've been holding off because of perfection?
2. List one thing that you can tweak today to make it better. Example: your social media post or a section of your chapter in your book.
3. List one thing that perfection has stopped you from doing. Example: writing your own book, doing a LIVE on social media, or reaching out to an influencer.

To access the action plan and materials for this chapter, go to:

https://www.izdiharjamil.com/resources

Investing

"Investing in yourself doesn't stop. It's how you grow!"

— Dr. Izdihar Jamil

One of the ways that you can grow your business exponentially is by investing. Investing in what, you might ask? First and foremost, invest in yourself because for things to change, you must change first.

Investing in Yourself

Your inner world creates your outer world. And your inner world starts with who you are, your thoughts, and your being. Like I've mentioned in the previous chapter, you have to be able to grow. If you're not growing, you're dying.

In order for you to grow, you have to invest in yourself. Whether you're learning a new skill set, investing in your health and wellness or an infrastructure that can help to expand your business, it starts with planting the seeds and taking the time to nurture what's necessary.

One of the ways that you can rapidly grow is by hiring or investing in a coaching program or a system. Basically, you're hiring someone who is a few steps ahead of you, and who can help you get from where you are now to where you want to be.

When you're fighting for your dreams and taking courageous steps every day toward it, you don't want to be reaching out to people who are a few steps back from you. How are they supposed to guide you when they haven't been there themselves? What you need is an expert eye that can tell you very quickly and effectively on how to tweak things, so you can hit your dreams faster than you thought possible.

The right person will show up once you are ready to commit to your dreams. For example, my dream is to be the best *TED* speaker. I didn't know how I was going to do that. On top of that, speaking on stage scares me big time. But I chose to commit to my dreams and stay loyal to it.

Then Michelle Mehta, who was one of my clients, came along and said, *"Izzy, you should be a* TEDx *speaker and I'll support you!"*

She's a *TEDx* speaker herself and her dream was to have me speaking on the *TEDx* stage. She held me accountable and held the space for me when I had my tantrums and rejections.

Next came Bo Eason, who is one of the best storytellers and stage performance coaches that I have ever met. He was an NFL player, and he knew what it takes to be the best and win championships. After his career in the NFL, he trained to be a stage actor and has performed over 1300 performances. He taught me about the art of storytelling and how to be magnetic on stage.

Then there were many other incredible people that have helped me practice my *TED* Talk and gave me ideas to tweak it to make it better. But it starts with you making a bold declaration of your dreams and the commitment to invest in yourself to make your dreams come true. The right person will show up at the *divine* timing.

My dreams came alive on 4th December 2021 when I presented my talk at the prestigious *TEDx* Del Throne Women stage in Los Angeles, California. I practiced relentlessly for my talk and gave my heart out on the day. I had the longest and the loudest standing ovation of the day, and my dreams came true.

To see my *TED* Talk on *"Coming to America: A Story of a Hijab Wearing Woman",* go to *TED.com* and search for Izdihar Jamil. It's only 8 minutes and 11 seconds long but it has been dubbed as a profound and a heart touching talk. Sonali Fiske, the curator of the *TEDx Del Throne Women*, called me *"A Master Storyteller".*

As a result, my credibility as the #1 go-to expert in my field skyrocketed because of my association with a prestigious platform. Many people and organizations have reached out and asked if I can give a talk at their institutions. Clients are also saying YES to working with me because of my commitment to my dreams.

So whatever your dreams are, start investing in yourself first. Allow the right people to help you fight for your dreams. The only way that your dreams aren't going to come true is when you quit. But know this, darling, that when your dreams come alive, it sets a trickling effect for other people to make a positive shift in their lives, too. How can you not fight for your and their dreams?

In your business, whatever your goal or dream is, for example, being the best salesperson, being the best performance coach, learn from people who are the best at what they do. Make sure that they are already a few steps ahead of you. More importantly, make sure that you're in alignment with them. Feel their vibe.

Those who truly want to see you successful will never crush your dreams, or tell you to take a step back, or tell you that you're not ready yet. Once they know what your dream is, they'll do everything they can to help you make it happen.

Remember, you're the prize, so you get to choose the best person to be in your team.

Doing the work

Once you've invested in yourself, in a coach, or in a system, what people are often expecting is for the results to show up miraculously with little effort. Yes, miracles do happen, but only and only when you have given everything that you have and all there is left to do is to surrender.

It's the same with you. Once you've made the investment, the other part of the equation that people often ignore is doing the work every day. Action produces results. By being in action, it's the bridge that's going to connect you with your knowledge and the results that you desire.

For example, I wanted to be good at sales. So I listened to various audible books from experts, took courses, and hired coaches to help me. All that isn't going to make much of a difference until I'm actually doing the sales call itself. Being in reality or being on the ground doing the fieldwork itself is different from theoretical perspectives.

What got me better and better at doing sales calls is engaging in thousands of sales calls over the years and mastering the art of selling and conversion that is based on the meeting of the hearts.

So when I invest in something, I do the work. I'm committed to the work. And doing that, I not only make the money back, but I also make profits from it. I actually have the opportunity to help others.

When you invest in something and you're committed to the work, you're going to get a return on investment. It's the same thing, like when you have a garden, you put the effort in; you water it; you fertilize it, and you take care of it. You put the work in, and in result, the plants grow and give you the fruits.

It's the same thing in business. So you have to invest first and foremost in yourself and then do the work. If you're truly, truly committed to the work and your dreams, your investments will pay off. It's that predictable.

Power Summary

Let's review the key points in this chapter.

1. What's one way that you can grow your business?
2. What do you need to do to get the results after making an investment?
3. Fill in the blank. Hire a coach, consultant, or a system that is ____________________.

Key Actions

Here are your steps to help you move forward in your business.

1. List one of your biggest dreams this year.
2. List one expert that you feel can help you.
3. Reach out to that person and have a conversation with them to see if you're a good fit to work together.

To access the action plan and materials for this chapter, go to:

https://www.izdiharjamil.com/resources

Simple

"Simple is the best! The simpler things are, the more effective you become."

— Dr. Izdihar Jamil

When I was attending the *Make Your First Million: Female Entrepreneurs Retreat* in Bali, Indonesia, I met with Vanessa Moss, who is an incredible female entrepreneur. She's a 7-figure earner and also a mom of six. She's been featured on *Forbes*, Fox TV, and other influential media. She has taught me how to build my business using effective and simple methods.

One day as I was swimming, Vanessa came closer toward me at the edge of the pool and we were just hanging out. As we were chatting, she said, *"The biggest thing that I can tell you about running a business is to keep things simple."*

A lot of times, you tend to overcomplicate things and make it difficult for you to get the results quickly.

She said that by keeping things simple, she was able to build a successful business. For example, as I've shared in my previous chapter, my client conversion system is really simple—it's just ABC. Attract-Book-Convert. I've mastered the arts of organic lead generation, hence one less thing to deal with any paid advertisements. When I first started, I didn't have any websites.

When you've stripped down all the sparkly objects and the fluffy stuff, you realize that you actually need only a few things to build a business. Once you've mastered those few fundamental things, you'll realize that your business will explode because of your mastery.

When you keep things simple and let go of unnecessary factors, you can move things faster and become more effective. There's a saying *"How can you make the boat go faster?"*

It isn't about adding more things, it's about what are the things that you can take away to make it go lighter and faster.

The same in your business. Ask yourself the following questions as a guideline:

- What can you take out to streamline your business? It can be a process, a software, a system, or anything that you can think of.
- If you can only do one thing and one thing only to get a particular result, what would that one thing be?
- Who do I need to let go to help make my business grow faster?
- How can I make it easy for my clients to say YES to me?
- How can I simplify my methods so my clients can get results faster and with ease?

One of the things that I do while helping female leaders in becoming the go-to expert in their fields is that I help them to become a bestselling author. The biggest feedback that I've received from my clients is that I made it so easy and simple for them to be an author.

Afterwards, I even teach them on how they can leverage their book so they can grow their business. So think about how you can make it easy for your clients to get results. Think about how they just need to focus on one thing alone and the rest be outsourced or eliminated.

Just One Thing

Previously, I used a software called SamCart to create my sales pages and take payments from my clients. It's quick and easy for me to do, and I can usually whip out a sales page within minutes. However, using SamCart has a few setbacks, such as it takes the experience of my clients to a third party, which may impact the trust-credibility factor with my customers. Also, it's costing me an additional expense to maintain the membership of using that software.

But I always had a vision of maintaining my customer experience from my brand and my website. So I figured out how I can create a sales page from my own website and integrate online payment from it. Now, everything is being streamlined into one system—my website. I don't need additional software and expenses because of the simplification.

How cool is that, right?

You can check out one of my top services that I've designed for female leaders who want to grow their business rapidly through conscious PR and publicity. It's what I call my Diamond package here: www.izdiharjamil.com/diamond and see how I have created the sales page into my website and integrated the payment within my website too.

Faster Results

One of the things that I've noticed recently is the need for clients who want to get results faster and in the simplest way. Majority of my clients are busy women, often juggling between a successful business, family, and community. The time they have needs to be used wisely on the things that are important to them. However, there are certain things that they desire for their business but haven't got much time to do it themselves.

That's where I come in.

What I'm the best at is helping female leaders to share their voices on prestigious platforms around the world without prejudice. I do this by leveraging conscious PR and publicity methods that are in alignment with their dreams and values.

For example, if my client wants to get featured on *Forbes*, rather than teaching them how to pitch and then would have to do it themselves, I would put them in a face-to-face meeting with a Senior *Forbes* writer so they can get directly in front of the right person.

If they want to get on TV and magazines, I'll take care of everything for them, such as pitching and building the connections, then all they have to do is just show up and share their stories. That way, their time is being used effectively because I have simplified the process for them.

Converting Copywriting

Part of your client attraction method is using social media to share about your vision, stories, transformation, and how you can help your ideal clients to get the results that they want. Having a converting copywriting to attract the best clients is key to your business success.

Again, simplicity plays a huge role in creating copywriting that converts. The best copywriting posts that I've designed are the ones with the simplest and shortest word count. For example:

PINCH ME.... My TED *Talk is out!*

Stay LOYAL to your dreams and it'll come ALIVE!

This one received hundreds of likes and comments.

Looking for Female Leaders to speak at the "Women Who Lead" summit. YES!

This one also received hundreds of likes and comments.

In terms of your copywriting for your business, social media, book, sales page, and marketing materials, think about how you can keep the words simple. How can you write it in just a few lines that will give the right impact? People don't have time to read long messages. Often, long and complicated messages can create confusion, and the confused mind never buys.

For example, on social media, your audience would only get to see the first few lines, and after that, they're going to need to *"click more"* to see the remainder of your text. So how can you capitalize on those few lines that will intrigue them or make them curious to learn more about you or your messages?

Everybody can write pages and pages of content, but it takes true mastery to write just a line that summarizes everything that you need to say. To do this, it starts with practicing with the intention of keeping things simple. Ask yourself, if I could only write this in just one line, what would that be?

Rather than beating around the bushes, often honesty and being straight to the point is the best way forward. All you're looking for is either a YES or a NO. If it's a YES, great! Take it to the next step in your process. If it's a NO, then that's great too, because you can then shift your focus on other people who're excited about your work.

Keep things intentional, short, and simple. For example:

Hey Sarah, :)

Quick question. Would you LOVE to get featured on TV in 30 days?

Izdihar

Now Sarah can either say YES or NO.

Can you see how simple I've made things? Simplicity is cash. That's how the best copywriters work—they keep things simple and straight to the point. You don't need 20-30 lines before getting to your message. Remember, if you can get it in one line, what would it be?

Minimum effort, maximum results. That's what you need to focus on.

Power Summary

Let's review the key points in this chapter.

1. Fill in the blank. Simplicity is ____________.
2. If you could do it online, what would it be?
3. Think about what are the things that you can eliminate in your business to simplify and streamline your business.

Key Actions

Here are your steps to help you move forward in your business.

1. Write 1-2 simple lines for your post on social media.
2. List down one thing that you can eliminate in your business to make the boat go faster. It can be a process, a system, or a project.
3. List one way that you can simplify your process to help your clients get results faster and easier.

To access the action plan and materials for this chapter, go to:

https://www.izdiharjamil.com/resources

"Simpler is the best! The simpler things are, the more effective you become."

— Dr. Izdihar Jamil

Procrastination

"Procrastination is just resistance in disguise. When you remove the resistance, you can beat procrastination."

— Dr. Izdihar Jamil

Procrastination is one of those things that will stop you from achieving your goals or making your dream happen. Putting things off for a timed period or an indefinite time frame is never healthy for your productivity.

There are many reasons for procrastination:

- Fear of failure. You feel that when you do it, there's a chance of failure, and that scares you.
- Fear of success. You feel that when you do it, you're not ready to handle the success that comes with it.
- It feels too big. You feel that a particular task feels too big and complicated that it's impossible to tackle.
- A resistance. A blocker that's stopping you from moving forward that could be from your past or present circumstances.
- You don't see the value of doing it or it's a repetitive task that does not challenge you.

Procrastination can be the biggest block in your ability to get the money that you desire in your business. If you don't figure out a way to break through the vicious cycle, it will hold you down and, over time, it'll turn into the scariest monster that's continuously haunting you.

Bypassing Procrastination

Over the years, as a mother, wife, a Ph.D. student, and an entrepreneur, I've learned various tricks to bypass procrastination. Here are my top tips that I've found effective in beating procrastination:

- Breaking down the task into a smaller checklist.
- Focus on conquering one item at a time.
- Use the golden rule of *"I touch things once"*, meaning that once you've touched it, quickly complete it.
- Let go of perfection and just start, even when you don't feel that you're ready.
- Reward and compliment yourself every time you've completed a task.

For example, I needed to create an email list sequence for those who attended my training. I usually do 7-9 email sequences, which can be overwhelming at times. So what I do is that I block my calendar for 1-2 hours just to focus on that task.

Then I'll focus on writing the first email in the simplest way possible and completing that. Then I'll work on the second email and then the next. Yes, there would be times when I couldn't complete the email sequence that I want.

When that happens, here are the things that I usually do:

- Create another block of time in the calendar for me to complete it.
- Re-adjust my strategy so that I'll complete the work as is though I may need to tweak some things to make it effective.
- Ask another team member to help me out.

The same methods can be applied to other parts of your business and projects. For example, in writing this book, I asked a team member to help me clean up my notes and draft.

Then I blocked my calendar and booked myself at a hotel so I can focus on polishing my work for 48 hours without my family, so that I can fully concentrate on my work. All I did was focus on completing one chapter and then the next and the next. Afterwards, I asked another team member to help edit and publish it.

I Touch Things Once

I've lightly touched on this concept at the beginning of this chapter. The simplest way to explain this concept is that once I touch something, I will quickly finish it there. This means I don't have to come back to it a second or third time, which in turn increases my productivity.

For example, I wanted to do an *Instagram* reel on my profile. Rather than saying later, when I've got to have the perfect outfit and when I've done my makeup, I would take my camera and just do it "as is", in my existing outfit and environment.

By letting go of perfection, I get to tick off one more thing on the plate. Often the "later" either never happens or becomes an add-on to more things that I have to do on my checklist.

In another example, when I open an email and read it, rather than responding to it later, I would respond to it right away even if it's just a few sentences. What usually happens is that I forget to respond to that email as more things come into my plate. Now the trick here is to block out a time when you check your emails because the last thing you want is to be replying to emails all day long.

Team Effort

The last thing that can help you beat procrastination is by having a team to support you. For example, I had a vision of creating my own magazine. Yes, I can do my own design, but I neither have the time nor the skilled expertise to make the magazine look aesthetically pleasing.

So rather than the idea of just sitting there waiting for me to do it, I hired a graphic designer to help me design the magazine and make my vision come alive. As a result, Spotlight Female Entrepreneurs Magazine was born!

You can check out the magazine here:

https://www.izdiharjamil.com/spotlight-magazine

Yes, hiring a team member means additional costs. But the benefits of hiring a team member who can do the job well outweigh the costs. It also means that you get to free your time to do more important things that you love doing.

Power Summary

Let's review the key points in this chapter.

1. What's one reason people procrastinate?
2. What's one tip that I gave that can beat procrastination?
3. How can hiring a team member help to beat procrastination?

Key Actions

Here are your steps to help you move forward in your business.

1. List one thing that you have been procrastinating.
2. List one small action plan that you can do today that you've been procrastinating about.
3. List one reward for yourself that you're going to enjoy once you've conquered your task.

To access the action plan and materials for this chapter, go to:

https://www.izdiharjamil.com/resources

Follow Up

"The fortune is in the follow up."

— Dr. Izdihar Jamil

I remember I had this one client. When I offered my services to her, she said "*No*". After some time, I followed up with her and offered to help her in her business. She said "No". This pattern kept on happening several times until one day she said "Yes!" and made the payment.

At one point, only 3% of people are ready to buy. So if you don't follow up, you're missing 97% of the potential sales. Majority of entrepreneurs give up after the first-time people say "no".

I was like that too. When I got a "no" the first time from a potential client, I said, *"If she doesn't want to work with me, that's fine. I'll look for someone else!"*

But actually, that person has already expressed an interest, but for some reason wasn't ready at that moment. By consistently reaching out and nurturing them, you're solidifying your relationship with them.

Rejection is a blessing. It's just a correction toward your destined success. There will be a point when things just click and it's a YES!

There's been many times when someone says NO for this particular project but then says a YES for another project. Sometimes it may lead to a new collaboration. Or that person might refer someone to you because they trust you.

All you need to do is plant the seeds and continue nurturing it. Your efforts are never wasted. For example, I have a lady who said No to my offer to help her in her authority building but bought my book. I've got influencers who collaborate with me on my project and ended up buying a copy of my magazine. Then they recommend me to others for me to help them.

So keep on following up and nurture your leads with authenticity and love and something good always will come back to you.

Two Types of Follow Up

There are two kinds of followup. The front-end follow up is for the new people who haven't worked with you before but have expressed an interest in working with you. Here are some of the ways that you can entice them:

- Offer them something small at an affordable price so they can have confidence in your system. This can be one of the modules in your course.

- Do an irresistible bonus offer that you know is something that they're interested in, for example, when clients invest in my media and publicity package, they'll get a photoshoot with a top branding photographer when they pay in full.

- Slash the price of the offer that you know they are interested in, but only if they pay in full, and it's only for a limited time period, like a flash sale of 24 hours.

- Invite them to purchase your book if they have financial difficulties. Often, people are able to invest in a $10 book.

- Offer them a FREE 45-minute group training and Masterclass session before upselling them to your products and services.

The back-end follow up is for your existing clients, and you upsell them to the next level of their journey. Statistics show that once someone has bought something from you, they are 80% more likely to buy it from you again. In order for you to upsell, you need to have your product stacks available.

What you want to think about is the next thing that they want on their journey.

For example, clients who have completed an anthology book project with me may want to write their own solo book, create their own anthology book, or get featured in the media to share their message. So I have prepared the exact packages to help them with their dreams and the next journey that they want to take.

So plan out your client's next move in order for them to make their dreams come true. Often it's a similar path to the ones that you have taken. For example, in building my business and positioning myself as the #1 go-to expert in my field, I have:

- Become a #1 international bestselling author multiple times.
- Been featured on hundreds of media including FOX, NBC, and CBS.
- Been featured on TV.
- Been featured on the front cover of global magazines.
- Been featured on the iconic *Forbes* platform.
- Been featured on the prestigious *TED* stage.
- Been interviewed on many high-profile podcasts.
- Been speaking on prestigious stages around the world.

Because I have gone through those journeys myself, I know that's what my clients want and so my product and services are designed to help my clients fulfil those dreams.

Nurture Your Clients

One of my biggest tips in turning a "no" into a "yes" is to listen to what your clients are saying, and then tweak your offer. Follow up with them on a consistent basis. Keep dropping things that are in alignment with them and keep answering any of their concerns or queries.

For example, once a client was like, *"Oh, writing a book is a shiny object."*

I understand that's what they want, so I give them the space to think things through. I also said that writing a book can help you attract the best clients because you're instantly seen as the expert. Also, my clients have made $20K and more by leveraging their book. Will that help you with your business?

Make things easy for them and help them feel at peace with their concerns. Often, fear is one of the biggest things that's going to stop them. Your job is to continue to be there for them, care for them, and make them feel important. That's how you're going to win them.

If payment is their biggest obstacle, let them know that you're willing to work with them to make things easy for them. You can take things out of your products so it'll reduce the investment. You can offer them a payment plan to help spread out the cost. You can also slash out the price or offer a scholarship, but only if they pay within 24 hours.

All you need is to be creative in solving the problems and creating a win-win between you and them. Ask them, *"What's the most important thing that you want? We can figure it out together!"*

People want to feel valued. They want to be treated like they matter, despite their challenges. So take care of them just like how you'll take care of your family members, and you'll win them every time.

Power Summary

Let's review the key points in this chapter.

1. Fill in the blank. The fortune is in the _____________.
2. What are the two types of follow up system that I mentioned?
3. What's my biggest tip in turning a "no" into a "yes"?

Key Actions

Here are your steps to help you move forward in your business.

1. Make a list of 5 people that you can do a follow up with.
2. List down your offer for them based on their desires.
3. List down one thing that you can add/remove from your offer to create a win/win for both of you.

To access the action plan and materials for this chapter, go to:

https://www.izdiharjamil.com/resources

Heart

"The heart never lies. It's your true guiding compass."

— Dr. Izdihar Jamil

Oprah Winfrey once said that one of the reasons that she made mistakes was when she wasn't listening to her heart. I've interviewed many successful people for my Podcast *Yes I Can!* and my book projects and listening to your heart is one of the most common themes that successful people have.

As an entrepreneur, we sometimes bypass our hearts and just focus on the logic part of the business. While this can be an important factor, sometimes even though the numbers look right, there's just something missing. And the heart knows this.

For example, I had a call with this client. While talking to him, his credentials fit the profile of a good candidate for my program. However, the way he talked, the questions he asked, and the 'vibe' that he was giving me felt off. But I bypassed that feeling and accepted him into my program.

As the program went along, I had to give him a lot of attention, more than I did for my other clients. He would create unnecessary friction with me. That took a lot of time and energy, taking care of the situation.

From the first moment, my heart knew that we were not a good fit despite it being a logical decision. It wasn't because he wasn't a good person; it was just that we operated differently. The best things that have happened to me is when I listen to my heart no matter if it sounds crazy. So now I would use my heart as my guiding compass to make my decisions in my personal life and business.

Be Kind to Yourself

Often, we are the toughest on ourselves. We demand too much of ourselves and when things don't go our way; we blame ourselves for the failure. What I have learned is to be kind, compassionate, and to love myself. Just like your child, you need to be nurtured and taken care of, too.

When you feel that you're getting tired, rather than pushing yourself, it's OK to say that *"You've done a good job. Let's take a break and we can continue tomorrow!"*

Imagine yourself as a six-year-old. What would you say to that little six-year-old you when you've done so much work but at the end, someone is putting that little six-year-old you down because they haven't done enough? Think about it for a moment.

Wouldn't you want someone to be kind and loving toward you and appreciate you, no matter what?

Absolutely!

It's the same with you. The more loving, kind, and generous you are with your current self, the more confident and successful you'll become. The best way for you to thrive is when you're in a loving and nurturing environment. And that starts with being kind to yourself.

Me Time

Often, we take care of everyone around us to the point of exhaustion and then completely ignore our own needs and desires. That's why self-care is so important, even if it's just 5 minutes for yourself.

Me time doesn't just happen. You have to create the space for it. For example, schedule it in your calendar or communicate it with your family that between 9-10 p.m. every day is your time.

For me, my time is around 5 a.m. in the morning, where I'll start off by doing my prayers and reading the Quran to ground myself spiritually. After breakfast and dropping the kids off at school, I usually like to take a walk with my baby in my neighborhood and walk barefoot in my garden.

After lunch, I usually like to spend a few minutes just sitting at the dining table before continuing my day. At night, after my baby falls asleep, I would spend that time watching some funny videos on YouTube or reading a book before sleeping.

Once a year, I like to take what I call a Mommy-only trip and create it as part of my business. In 2019, I traveled to London to give a lecture at Sussex University and attended a training. In between those, I get to rest and chill on my own. In 2021, I booked myself for two nights at a hotel to finish writing this book without the kids.

There are many ways that you can create your *me time* throughout the day. My best tip for you is to start small and build your routine as you consistently honor your *me time*.

Power Summary

Let's review the key points in this chapter.

1. Fill in the blank. The heart never ____________.
2. Why do you need to be kind and loving to yourself?
3. Other than your logic, what can you use as your guiding compass?

Key Actions

Here are your steps to help you move forward in your business.

1. In which area of your life today can you use your heart as your guiding compass?
2. List one way that you can be kind to yourself today.
3. List one thing that you can do during your me time today.

To access the action plan and materials for this chapter, go to:

https://www.izdiharjamil.com/resources

Heart

"The heart never lies. It's your true guiding compass."

— Dr. Izdihar Jamil

Money Management

"Set the intention of every penny that comes your way and you will feel the blessings that it brings."

— Dr. Izdihar Jamil

Every penny that comes into your life is a blessing. It has a purpose and a soul. Honor it by acknowledging its presence and setting the intention for each penny. The flow of money is such that it'll come and go. It comes to your life to nourish you, take care of you, and when it leaves your life, it's meant to help others too.

Ken Honda in his book *Happy Money* said that one of the best ways to create a happy movement in your money is by saying *Thank you* when the money comes in and also by saying *Thank you* when the money goes out.

Majority of the time people say *Thank you* when the money reaches their accounts, but when it leaves, it causes anxiety and stress because of the "lack of" or "less" mentality. Meaning that you'll have less money in the bank when you have to spend it.

By saying *Thank you* when the money comes in and goes out, it'll create a positive and happy energy flowing in and out of your bank account. That, in turn, will attract more money into your life because of your appreciation attitude.

Think of it this way, when your manager gives you a bonus and you're so appreciative and perform better in your job. You often thank him for his kindness in giving you a bonus. Now compare it with someone who says, *"The bonus is just too little!"* or complains about it. Who would your manager rather choose to give the bonus again—you or the complainer? That's right, YOU.

So the happy movement starts with saying *Thank you* when the money comes in and goes out of your bank account. Say it every day, several times a day. Then observe how the quality of your life changes.

Money is just the result of YOU. Who do you choose to be in your relationship with money? That's right, you and money have a relationship. Just like how you have a relationship with your parents, spouses, children, and the people around you.

Imagine money as your best friend. Would your best friend want to hang out with you when you're moody, grumpy, angry, and complaining all the time? Yup, money will run away.

Now imagine that when your best friend comes, you laugh, smile, love, and have so much fun with her and treat her so special. Would she want to come back and love you? Absolutely! Treat money with love, kindness, respect, and honor, and it'll come back to you multifold.

Software and Team

First of all, as a business owner and entrepreneur, you need to have an accounting software that's going to help you take care of your accounting. It is going to help make things easy for you to see your profit and loss, balance sheets, assets, and for your accountant or CPA to manage things for you.

Right from the beginning, you keep things organized and streamlined so that you'll know exactly where you stand in terms of your business health. You can also see how you can improve your business and know exactly where you stand with your numbers. When it comes to the tax season, everything is easy and ready for you to present to your accountant.

Remember, your numbers tell you a story, so listen to it. It's telling you what it needs, what needs to be added, removed, and what it loves the most. For me, I usually have at least one meeting with my accountant throughout the year to check where I'm at with my business health.

We look at strategies to increase my profits and savings into my bank account. So if you haven't arranged a meeting yet with your accountant, I recommend that you do it within the next 24-48 hours.

Hiring the best accountant and tax advisor saves me a lot of money in my business. It takes the stress of having to do it myself and doing it correctly. My accountant Ronica Brown also guides me in thoroughly planning my money so I can increase my profits and savings.

I also have a bookkeeper that keeps my accounting up to date. Often freelancing bookkeepers and accountants offer good value in terms of services and hiring costs. Plus, you're not left with any headache of having an employee since they are contractors. You can look for many skilled and talented freelancers on Fiverr or Upwork.

Even though your bookkeeper does an excellent job in keeping track of your records, you still need to check through their work and make sure that the numbers are correct. I've had instances where my bookkeeper made a mistake of classifying certain items which lead to an incorrect financial health of my business. That caused unnecessary stress. The numbers in your business are your responsibility. Learn how to read them so that you're always on top and it makes it difficult for people to cheat on you.

To keep track of my business accounting, I use a software called Quickbooks. There are many types of software out there, such as Zero and Quickbooks that you can use. I personally use Quickbooks, because in America, it's one of the most popular software, and also because my accountant and bookkeeper are pretty familiar with it.

It's easy to set up. I just took the starter page, as that's all that I need. I can see my profits and loss, balance sheets, assets and liabilities. I can also issue an invoice and create ongoing payment using the software.

Within a few clicks, I can see the health of my business and what I need to do to keep in health and in the blacks. Your accountant should be able to teach you how to read your numbers and the adjustments that you need to make.

As a business owner, I highly recommend that you set up a business account that's separate from your personal account. Don't mix those two as it'll be really messy. The separation also gives you clarity on your numbers, and clarity leads to power. For tax purposes, you can clearly expense certain items and expenses under the business costs.

A quick tip: If you want to open a business account, you need to have some form of entity. In America, it's called an LLC or Limited Liability Company, or it can be a corporation partnership, etc. But you have to create an entity for your business, not only for the purpose of opening accounts but also for the purpose of tax, protection, and for many other reasons. Speak to your financial advisor to find out which type of entity is the best for you.

Money Management

Since 2009, I have been using the same money management system where I like to create separate accounts for my money. Each account has its own purpose.

In my business, I have created three accounts in total. You can have more if you want. But I have three at the moment and that's enough for me. I want to keep it as simple as possible by managing three business accounts.

The first account is the main account. We call it the checking account in America. The purpose of the checking account is what I call the necessity. I use it to pay for all my necessities associated with running my business, for example, paying software companies for my business, paying for contractors, paying for business trips, etc.

The second account that I have is what I call the profit and growth account. The purpose of this account is for me to keep aside an amount monthly that I want to save for expansion and the growth of my business.

And then the third account is called a tax account. And it does exactly what it's named after. The purpose of the account is to hold on to the money that is needed for any tax or licensing purposes.

In business, you would only pay the taxes at the end of the year, after you have made the expenses. This is different if you're an employee because as an employee, the first thing that's going to be taken out of your paycheck is the tax, and then you'll get the remainder.

But for business owners, it's completely the opposite. You would incur the expenses first and then what is left of your money, the tax is paid with that. So you want to be prepared for that because you want to make sure that you have enough funds to pay for your tax.

The Structure

This is how I structure my finances when money comes in.

Step #1: Set a date

I would set a date on the day that I will be doing my accounting. It's like having a date with a friend. I would book this date on my calendar. This is the day that I'm spending time to look at my finances and clear off invoices. Mine is usually on the 30th of every month.

Step #2: Pay yourself first

The #1 rule of money—always, always pay yourself first. That's what I do. I pay myself first. Commonly, people would pay off their debt, mortgage, credit cards, and whatever is left, they'll put in their savings account. Often there isn't much left in the account.

I would go the opposite way of paying myself first no matter what and then take care of the bills. By doing this, I make sure that I take care of myself first. I've been doing this for over a decade and for some mystical reason, I always have more money left over to pay for other people. So trust in the process.

Step #3: Give to Charity

You would always want to give back and share the blessing that you're receiving with other people. Help take care of your community, and you will see that it's a profitable investment that always comes back to you multifold. There's something about seeing the joy in your community, knowing that you've played a part in causing it. It's also a great tax saving strategy.

You can give whatever amount you want. Just commit to a number and then stick to that. My commitment is a minimum 2.5 percent of what I get. It goes to several charities of my choice. You are welcome to give more. I even have a standing order for this tithing to happen automatically from my necessity account.

Step #4: Profits & Growth and Tax Account

The step is transferring a certain amount to my profits and growth account, as well as my tax account. I want to make sure I have the funds ready for me to go for my dreams, as well as putting some money aside for tax purposes. I usually set about 20% of my income for each account.

The amount isn't fixed forever. As a business owner, I know our business fluctuates. So you can always change the figure accordingly. The key here is to transfer the money consistently every month, and you'll see it grow every time.

Step #5: Payment

Once I've taken care of paying myself, charity, and my profits and tax accounts, then and only then would I take care of my bills and outstanding invoices. You have to trust in the abundance and in the process. Somehow, it always works out.

If you need to, you can adjust the numbers and take some from your other accounts to take care of the bills.

Top tip: Never leave your bank account at $0. Always, always leave some money in the bank because money attracts money. You're setting the container ready for it to welcome more by leaving some wealth in it.

Power Summary

Let's review the key points in this chapter.

1. What are the three business accounts that I have?
2. What's the first thing that I do once I receive the money?
3. Say *Thank you* when the money comes and *Thank you* when the money leaves your account to create the *Happy Money* movement.

Key Actions

Here are your steps to help you move forward in your business.

1. Set up an appointment with your accountant within the next 24-48 if you haven't done so for this year to review your financial health. If you don't have one, hire one. You can check out my accountant, Ronica Brown at (https://rbataxadvisors.com/).
2. Pay yourself first this month and make a commitment to do so every month.
3. Give in to charity this month and make a commitment to do so every month.

To access the action plan and materials for this chapter, go to:

https://www.izdiharjamil.com/resources

The Queen Mindset

"Tell yourself Yes I Can! And so it is done!"

— Dr. Izdihar Jamil

At every turning point, your fears, glass ceilings, and self-limiting beliefs are going to come creeping in and stop you from taking the next step. I've seen this myself, in my clients and as well as in the people around me. Be aware of this "trap". When this happens, you'll have the choice to either pull back, stay the same, or push through. Whichever one that you choose, remember that it has an impact on your life.

For example, a client from one of my book projects reached out to me and said, "*I can't do this, I want to pull back. I don't think I've got anything worthy to say.*"

First, know that this is totally normal and appropriate. Of course, you are going to freak out and get scared because this is totally outside of your comfort zone.

Celebrate this moment because it means that you're growing. It means that you're living! Rather than fixing it, just let it BE. Use that energy and then transform it into words in your book or into the work that you do. It's dynamic, it's the best thing about you, so use it as your fuel.

What I believe in is to fight for people's dreams, so when I speak to my clients, which is exactly how I'm going to demand from them—their greatness in making their dreams come alive. The only way for your dreams to not happen is if you quit on them.

When I set my dreams, whether it's being on *Forbes*, *TED*, Oprah, I want people to have the best people in my team who will help me make it happen. I have no space or time for dream crushes. That's how I treat my clients, as if their dreams were mine.

Having the right mindset is key in planting the right seeds for your success. Having the best team and the most effective system are also important ingredients to the manifestation of your dreams coming alive.

The best team will create the safest place for you to be, grounding and nurturing the space for you even when you're at your lowest. Then pull you back up so you can stand in your power. An effective system will create the structure for you to take the emotion out and just follow through the process.

All you're doing is taking a step closer to your dreams every time and soon your dreams and you will meet at a *divine* timing.

Queen Mindset

Often, I see that even though clients and colleagues have the best system and team but have a "poor" mindset. They are often frozen and don't get the results that they desire. Having a strong and positive mindset, or what I call as the "Queen Mindset" is one of the most crucial fundamentals to your success.

The "Queen Mindset" is a learnable skill. Here are some tips that I have found useful to lay the foundation for a strong Queen Mindset:

- Be aware of your current mindset. You can use a journal to write it down. Don't judge it, just allow it to flow.
- Acknowledge it and say "thank you" because that is what has kept you alive for all these years.
- Let it go. You can declare and say, *"I am open to healing and to letting it go because this is a conflict to my purpose."*
- Rewire your mindset by declaring positive affirmations that are in alignment with you. Some of mine are *"I'm the QUEEN in my QUEENDOM" and "I am the PRIZE"* and *"It Is Done"*.
- Continue to ground yourself in this new version of you by doing some breathing, prayers, walking barefoot in your garden, journaling, or tapping on a consistent basis.

Honor Your Word

There's a saying that goes "words create your world". Your word is that powerful. It has the ability to create and destroy your world. Be mindful of what you say, and when you do say something, honor it. Your word is law—it's precious and important.

When you make a promise but then break it, over time, you'll start to see that your words will have no weight or power in them. Your words would feel empty and hollow because a part of you knows that it's not going to happen.

Now I know that there are circumstances when it's just not possible to keep your word due to an unexpected emergency or natural disaster. If that happens, the key is to communicate it immediately to the people affected as soon as you know it.

For example, my best friend and I would talk every Tuesday. We have a mini-coaching session and we also hold each other accountable in our lives and creation. If for some reason either of us can't make it, we communicate to each other immediately. We either re-commit our conversation to a different time or do something simple like leave each other voice messages.

Nobody's perfect. Things happen in our lives. But rather than ignoring it and brushing it under the carpet, the game is how fast you can communicate and re-commit back to your words.

Goals or Dreams

I love setting goals and dreams, and I set them all the time throughout the year. Often some of my dreams come earlier than expected, so then I create a new set of dreams to help me move forward.

The best thing that I've learned in choosing my dream is to choose a dream that is the scariest, craziest, and most atrocious of all, rather than the one that is practical or doable. Because the scariest dreams are the ones that are going to demand you to be someone that you've never been before and make the greatness within you come alive.

Some of my scariest dreams that I have successfully manifested are to be featured on *Forbes*, *TED*, TV, high-profile magazines with the influencers, owning my own house, and many others.

Majority of people write their goals or dreams once a year, usually toward the end of the year or in the early part of January. But research shows that by the middle of January, a lot of those goals fail or are being abandoned. Darlings, the only way that your dreams are not going to come alive is when you quit on them.

One of the best ways that I've found to keep my dreams alive and on track is to write them repeatedly every day. If you can't do it every day, then make a commitment to write it at least on a weekly or monthly basis. If you can't even do that, at least review them on a consistent basis.

There are three rules for writing goals.

- First, you always start with an "I".
- Second, you always want to have a timeline for it, because that's the difference between goals and dreams. A goal is just a dream without a timeline, so always put in a timeline.
- And the third, you always put it in the present tense.

For example, I earn 10,000 dollars a month by the 30th of January 2021, or whatever that timeline is. Or, I have one hundred clients by the 30th of September 2021.

I earn, I make, I serve, I get, etc., whatever your goal is, whether in your business or in your personal life. And if you want to have help, I've created a goal setting that you can use to set your goals, so that you can check in with your goals every single day.

A top tip is to add "or more" to your dreams or use an adjective such as "the best" to give it an extra boost.

For example, I earn $100,000 or more a month by 30th January 2022 or I am the best *TED* speaker by 30 Dec 2021.

Trash Can Exercise

We have a lot of noises or disempowering beliefs within us. It can be because of our childhood, our past, trauma, or circumstances. One of the ways that I use to do the clearing of these unwanted noises is what I call the "Trash Can Exercise".

What does that exercise do? This exercise will help you to clean things up and trash out the unwanted things within your system. You can't build something good on top of rubbish. You have to clean it out first.

For example, if you have a garden full of weed, and you want to plant roses in it, the roses are not going to survive because the weed will use it all up. The only way for you to have a beautiful rose garden is for you to strip off all the weeds from the roots and make clear a setup of just soil.

You get rid of all the weeds, cleaning them out from the root, and then you plant the rose seeds. You then take care of it, nourish it, water it, and put fertilizers on it. You give it the sunlight, the love and care that it needs to grow into a beautiful rose garden. And as time goes, the roses will grow and bloom beautifully. That's the concept of a trash can.

You get to trash out the things that are not serving you so that you can create the best space for beautiful things to grow.

And how can you do this?

First, understand that everything is energy. It's the law of physics, that everything is energy. Energy cannot be killed. It can only be transferred or transformed.

What you need to do is to pull out all the negative energy and transform that into a high-performance energy that can serve you. Your fears, your pessimistic ideas, the noise, the chaos in your head, the insecurities, it's all stored within you. What you have to do is transfer or transform it.

Here's how you to do it:

- Take a piece of paper and a pencil.
- Transfer whatever emotions that you're feeling from your body to the pen and the paper, letting it all flow out. Just write whatever it is that you're feeling.
- It doesn't matter if you're feeling happy or insecure, whatever it is, just write it down. Don't judge it. Let it flow out. Just keep on writing.
- Write to the point that you begin to feel like you can't write anymore and to the point where you feel like there's a breathing space for you to breathe.
- When you come to that point, just take a deep breath and let go.

You may have to repeat this exercise a few times. You can do it at any time, at any moment. You can get it done as many times as you want. And once you've written that paper, just rip off that paper and trash it. It's no longer controlling you, and it's no longer within you.

Tell yourself, *I'm ready. I'm open to letting go. I'm ready to heal.*

And so it is.

Breathing Exercise

Another way to create the *"Queen Mindset"* is for you to do some breathing exercises. They only take a few minutes of your time. What you do is that you need to sit comfortably, let your shoulders relax, let your body relax, and close your eyes in a quiet space.

Take a deep breath in and a deep breath out. Breathe in and out. Repeat this several times until you've found a rhythm that you're comfortable with. There's nothing for you to do except to focus on your breath. Feel your breath moving in and out of you. All you have to do is just play some music in the background. You don't have to say the words or anything. Just focus on your breath. Do that for a few minutes, or however many minutes you want.

As you exhale, you let go of all the self-limiting belief that you were holding within. You tell yourself, *I'm letting go, I'm ready to heal.*

Once you're ready, come back to consciousness, and you'll feel a sense of calmness because your mind is quiet or settled as you breathe.

Journaling

Another idea that you can do to sharpen the "Queen Mindset" is to do some journaling.

There are various ways to do journaling. There's free flow journaling where you just dump everything and write whatever that you feel. You can also use structured or guided journaling or follow a process. There are many journals that offer this form of guided journaling.

What I found to be the most effective is to use a combination of both, like a middle ground. It's a loose structure but also has the ability to flow freely. The intention is to transform your thoughts and feelings from a low vibration energy to a high vibration energy, such as from anger to love.

Here's the five-step process that I use to do journaling:

- Start with a low vibration energy such as sadness, anger, frustration, and write it down.
- Allow for those feelings to be witnessed without judgement. You can say something like: *"I am allowing for these feelings to be witnessed."*
- Once those feelings have been acknowledged, make a decision to be open to healing. You can say something like: *"I am now open to healing it because it is a conflict"* or *"I choose to forgive..."*

- Then write down a few things that you are grateful for or the lessons that you've learned from those feelings or events that happened. You can say something like: *"I am grateful for..."*
- Finally, consciously choose to enter a state of happiness, joy, love, freedom, abundance, or any vision that comes into mind. You can say something like: *"I am now choosing to be..."*

Then observe how your body feels after this exercise. You may choose to repeat it several times and can do it as often as you want.

Celebration

To get to where you are now, there were hundreds or even thousands of things that needed to happen. For example, for you to have your food today, it had to be grown at a farm. Then someone had to pick it up, wash it, and pack it. After that, someone had to come and transport it from the farm to its destination, most likely at a store. Following that, an employee at a store had to stock it on the shelves. Then you would have to come to the store, buy it, and cook it before eating it.

Now how can we not be grateful and celebrate that success, right?

No matter how small you feel your success is, don't underestimate all the steps that you had to go through to achieve it. Celebrate the little success because those small victories are what lead you to winning your championships.

For example, my dream is to be the best *TED* speaker. I didn't even know how to apply to a *TED* event, let alone be a confident speaker. So I had to learn, talk to the right people, attend training, practice, pray, and do it all over again. Until on the 4th of December 2021, I presented my talk on the prestigious *TED* platform.

So along the way of my ups and downs, I celebrated because I know those things are just like lily pads that I needed to hop on to get to my desired destination.

Celebrating and rewarding your mini success doesn't have to be expensive. It can be as simple as taking a 5-minute walk in your garden or watching a funny video on YouTube. Here are some celebration ideas that I love:

- A walk in my garden or in my neighborhood.
- Watch a funny video on YouTube.
- Watch a movie on *Netflix*.
- Dressing up with any nice clothes that I have.
- Give myself a mini-facial.
- Put on a nice mask.
- Eat fruit or chocolate or whatever that I have in my kitchen.

If you can't celebrate the little things, you can't celebrate the big things. The big things only come when you've accomplished the little things, so it's important for you to celebrate the little things. Practice that muscle of celebration and reward, and you'll start to see how you get to enjoy the journey toward your destination.

Forgiveness

Now, the thing about a "Queen Mindset" is that forgiveness plays an important role in helping you move forward with power. If you don't forgive them, there is a sense of anger within you. Consciously or unconsciously, by being angry with someone, you're giving your power away to them even after years of the incident.

It's reclaiming your power back. It's time to shift the focus back to you! The only way for you to take back your power is by forgiving those people. There are three types of people that you want to forgive:

- Yourself.
- Your parents.
- Other people who have hurt you.

It starts by being kind and compassionate to yourself, by forgiving yourself first. Know that you are strong, beautiful, and brave. All the things that you have done are amazing, even when it seems like the biggest mistakes were never meant to hurt you or put you in the worst possible position. Just know that you always have your best interest at heart.

Then the forgiveness cycle moves to your parents, because your parents play one of the biggest roles in your growth. Whatever it is that your parents have done in the past, forgive them for it. Even though it can seem incomprehensible, just know that they have done the best that they could.

Finally, forgive those who have wronged you in the past. They may be acting out of their own survival mechanism or even their own unconventional belief system. Do not give them power over you. Forgive them. It's time for you to live your best life.

You can start your forgiveness rituals by saying or writing down the following prompts:

- *I forgive myself for doing this ___________. (event/circumstances)*
- *I forgive ______ (name of the person) for doing ________.*
- *I am freeing ________ (name of the person) from any wrong doings that they have done.*
- *I am free from _______ (event/circumstances) that _________ (name of the person) has caused.*
- *I am free.*

Forgiveness isn't important for them. Forgiveness is for you, so you can move on and live the life that you desire without anything holding you back.

I am Responsible

A lot of the time, we play the blame game. We become victims, like it's not our fault, it's theirs. What I want you to realize is that when you play the blame game, the person who is losing the most is you.

So rather than playing the victim, you need to step into the world of taking responsibility. Like rather than being a victim of other people's actions or circumstances, you take the responsibility of where you are in your life. You are responsible for your thoughts, feelings, actions, and non-actions.

When you play the blame game, you're putting someone down and putting yourself up as the winner. Imagine what it feels like to be on the other side of being the one to be blamed? It's a vicious feeling. So how can you get the things you want when you're causing pain to others?

For things to change, I must change first, so always bring the focus back to you and say, "*I am responsible. What can I create? What can I let go? What can I create to make things better?*"

It's not about being good, bad, right, or wrong. It's just about saying *"I am responsible",* and it cuts through the negative emotions that are circling around you.

When I first moved to America, I was faced with horrible social adversity. In my *TED Talk*, I shared how someone had literally thrown a bag of dog waste right on our doorstep for my daughter and me to discover. My daughter, Nadrah, was about 3 years old then, so you can imagine the impact and trauma that it had on both of us. You can watch my *TED Talk* by going to www.izdiharjamil.com.

For months I played the victim like,

"How can someone do this?"

"We did nothing wrong!"

"Society is messed up."

Guess what? This victim mentality only made me sick. I was living in fear. I didn't want to go out. I was crying all the time.

But the moment when I forgave those people, I let them go and shifted the power back to me, was the turning point in my life. I shifted my mindset from being a victim to being a creator in my life. I focused on things that are important to me, like building my business, my family, and my health. That's when things started to shift because what you focus on expands.

Declare the mantra that *"I am responsible"* and then shift your focus to what really matters. That's when you'll start planting the seeds for living your best life.

Tapping

I first discovered tapping in 2018 when I was co-teaching a course with a money coach. Tapping is a tool that is safe for the mind-body connection. I found that it's really helpful and effective in breaking through any mental barriers or emotions that I have. One of my favorite books on tapping is called *Tapping Into Wealth.*

The tapping process is similar to acupuncture. But instead of using needles, you just use two fingers and repeatedly tap them at certain points. Tapping has several points. You can check out the book *Tapping Into Wealth* to see the different tapping points. My favorite point is the one above your heart because whenever I feel stressed, my chest tightens. So that's the point that helps to release the tension.

What you do is that you take two fingers and tap through the points. When you start the tapping process, I would always recommend that you start by acknowledging how you're feeling at the moment. For example, "*I'm feeling angry. I'm feeling sad. I'm feeling sad but I don't know what this is and why this is happening to me.*"

Then the second part is that you choose to let go, choose to be open to healing. You can say something like: "*I'm open to healing. I'm letting it go. I'm ready to heal. I want this to be dissolved from my body.*"

The third phase is for you to create what it is that you want to happen or the feelings that you want to experience. You can say something like: "*I know that I'm a powerful woman. I'm the best at what I do. I know that I didn't make good choices in the past, but I'm ready to make good choices from now on. I'm committed to my choices. I am open to welcome the opportunities, the people, and new circumstances that can help me to be successful. I'm saying yes to myself.*"

Or whatever it is that you need to say to yourself at that moment.

Declaration

The last part of the "Queen Mindset" is the declaration. Declaration is powerful. It's like a prayer. Remember, your words create your world.

So don't underestimate the declaration. I remember one of my friends was saying, "*Oh, I hope they don't raise my rent by one hundred dollars!*" Guess what happens? Her rent was increased by a hundred dollars, exactly what's in her declaration.

What I want to say is that you need to have some affirmation, some declaration that you want to say over and over again to the point that it becomes reality. It's a way for you to rewire your mindset to create the life that you desire.

So whatever it is, create a list of a few powerful declarations that you can choose from. You choose to say all of them, one of them or a few of them. Here's a list of where you can start, and you can always add on as you go along.

I am a powerful creator.

I am an excellent money manager.

I'm an excellent receiver.

My income grows rapidly every day.

I have a large sum of money coming my way.

I deserve every success and opportunity that comes my way.

I step in and make the choices in my life.

I'm open to receiving goodness and welcoming more success and more money in my life.

Power Summary

Let's review the key points in this chapter.

1. What's one thing that you need to have to create a strong foundation for your Queen Mindset?
2. What's one method that you can use to sharpen your Queen Mindset? For example, journaling, meditation, prayer, etc.
3. Who are the three types of people that you need to forgive to bring the power back to you?

Key Actions

Here are your steps to help you move forward in your business.

1. List one positive declaration and say it out loud.
2. Say *I am responsible* three times.
3. Say I forgive _______ (the name of the person) three times.

To access the action plan and materials for this chapter, go to:

https://www.izdiharjamil.com/resources

Your Five-Step Action Plan

"Being in action is the only way for you to get the results that you desire."

— Dr. Izdihar Jamil

I know that we've covered a lot in this book, and you're probably left thinking, what's next? Or what's the best way for me to utilize the tools discussed in this book?

So here's my gift to you. I've stripped down everything from this book and laid out your five-step action plan on how you can have a money-making business without having to spend thousands of dollars on advertisements, a big following or complicated technology. Focus on mastering these five fundamentals, and you'll start to see results. Then you can add more steps as you feel more confident in your life and business.

Before we get into the five steps, declare your biggest, scariest, and most audacious dreams, and list them down.

Okay, now that we have a roadmap on where we're going, let's put the fundamentals on building your five steps toward scaling the business that you love.

Step #1: Queen Mindset

Choose 1-2 elements from the Queen Mindset that resonate with you and do them consistently. Some of the things that you can consider include:

- Prayer.
- Declaration.
- The Trash Can Exercise.
- Journaling.

- Tapping.

Step #2: Authority

Build your authority and position yourself as the #1 go-to expert in your field. Here's a checklist that you can use to navigate your authority building journey:

- Bestselling author.
- Media.
- TV.
- Magazines, and if possible, on the front cover of a global magazine.
- High-profile publications such as *Forbes, Entrepreneur, Business Insider*, Oprah.
- ted platform.
- High-profile podcast interviews.
- Speaking engagements.

Step #3: Your Non-Negotiable

Write down one of your most important non-negotiable in your personal and business life. For example, in your personal life, your non-negotiable is that you'll meditate every day. For your business life, your non-negotiable is that you are posting on social media every day to attract clients.

Keep things simple by starting with one first, and then add more as your muscles become stronger.

Step #4: Simplicity

Reflect on your life and business. Think about what are the things that you can take away to simplify it so that you're more effective in what you do. Just think about *"If I can take away only one thing, what will it be?"*

For example, is there a process that you can remove so your clients can get the results faster? Can you free up your time by hiring a housekeeper or a cook?

Step #5: Follow Up

The fortune is in the follow up. Create a simple but consistent follow up system to nurture both your leads and your existing clients. Remember, you can upsell or down-sell or start with something basic like offer your book to them.

I hope that you've found the methods that I have shared useful. They are not some theories that I've read but are real-life methods that I use in my own business as well as what I've taught my clients to do. Top tip: Make sure you invest in learning from the best so you can be the expert in what you do. Remember, the investment always comes back to you multifold.

I would love to hear how you're doing, what you love most about the methods that I've shared, and your success stories. You can find me on *Facebook, Instagram, LinkedIn*, and *Twitter* under Izdihar Jamil. Or email me at hello@izdiharjamil.com

Here's to your success and being the best version of you!

"Stay loyal to your dreams. Fight for it and it will come alive!"

— Dr. Izdihar Jamil

"Being in action is the only way for you to get the results that you desire."

— Dr. Izdihar Jamil

About the Author

Dr. Izdihar Jamil, Ph.D., is an immigrant, Asian, hijab wearing Muslim computer scientist turned media expert. She is a 10 x #1 International Bestselling Author of *It Is Done*, *Yes I Can!* And *Women Who Lead.*

Izdihar has spoken at many prestigious events and interviews all around the world. She was featured on *Forbes*, *TED*, Fox TV, NBC, CBS, ABC, CW, *Thrive Global*, and hundreds of media platforms and publications. In 2021, Izdihar was inducted into the prestigious Marquis *Who's Who* biography in recognizing her contribution as the top 5% in the industry alongside Warren Buffett and Oprah.

Her *TED Talk* on overcoming social adversity and the courage to be proud of her roots and heritage has inspired many people from various cultures to take a positive step toward accepting other people's principles and values.

Izdihar is an influential trailblazer and an inspirational leader in helping female leaders to share their voices on prestigious platforms without prejudice. She has helped over 100 female leaders to solidify their positions as the #1 go-to expert in their fields with her simple, no-fuss methods.

Izdihar lives in California with her husband and three kids, and in her spare time, she loves reading and baking for her family.

Contacts

Website: www.izdiharjamil.com

Social media: @iamdrizhiharjamil

Email: hello@izdiharjamil.com

Facebook: https://www.facebook.com/iamdrizdiharjamil

Instsgram: https://www.instagram.com/iamdrizdiharjamil/

LinkedIn: https://www.linkedin.com/in/iamdrizdiharjamil

Twitter: https://twitter.com/IzdiharJamil

Bestselling Books:

Full List: https://www.*Amazon*.com/dp/B08DBHD4HX
Women Who Lead : https://www.amazon.com/Women-Who-Lead-Timeless-Inspiring/dp/179488534X

FREE Training: How to become the #1 Celebrity Expert and explode your business! https://www.izdiharjamil.com/fast-authority

www.ingramcontent.com/pod-product-compliance
Lightning Source LLC
Chambersburg PA
CBHW051540170526
45165CB00002B/820

* 9 7 8 1 4 5 8 3 8 3 1 5 0 *